Revelations

In Memoriam of

The Six Hundred Years Anniversary

of

Saint Birgitta of Sweden

a special edition of the

Revelations

is bestowed by

Conrad Hilton

a man of vision and action

whose love and admiration for Saint Birgitta

generously sustained

The Ecumenical Foundation of America

❖

JULY 23, 1373: ROME 〜〜〜 LOS ANGELES: JULY 23, 1973

Our Father in Heaven

We pray that You save us from ourselves.

The world that You have made for us, to live in peace,

we have made into an armed camp.

We live in fear of war to come.

We are afraid of "the terror that flies by night and the arrow that flies by day,

the pestilence that walks in darkness and the destruction that wastes at noon-day."

We have turned from You to go our selfish way.

We have broken Your commandments and denied Your truth.

We have left Your altars to serve the false gods of money and pleasure and power.

Forgive us and help us.

Now, darkness gathers around us and we are confused in all our counsels,

losing faith in You, we lose faith in ourselves.

Inspire us with wisdom, all of us of every color, race and creed,

to use our wealth, our strength to help our brother, instead of destroying him.

Help us to do Your will as it is done in heaven

and to be worthy of Your promise of peace on earth.

Fill us with new faith, new strength and new courage,

that we may win the Battle for Peace.

Be swift to save us, dear God,

before the darkness falls.

—◆—

CONRAD HILTON

photo by Vladimir Novak

CONRAD HILTON

Knight Grand Cross with Collier of Merit

Paths of the Church

"WE want to give our assurance, once again,

that we have an attentive, reverent interest in the spiritual movements

linked with the problems of unity which are activating

vital and noble religious sentiments

in various individuals, groups and communities.

With love and reverence we greet all these Christians, in the hope

that we may further all even more effectively,

the cause of Christ and the unity He desired

for His Church, in the dialogue of

sincerity and love."

—◇—

HIS HOLINESS POPE PAUL VI

Revelations

With filial devotion to
HIS EMINENCE ALFREDO CARDINAL OTTAVIANI OF ROME
whose blessings and prayers inspired this work

Revelations

SAINT BIRGITTA OF SWEDEN

ANTHONY BUTKOVICH

ECUMENICAL FOUNDATION OF AMERICA

LOS ANGELES, CALIFORNIA

1973

Second Printing, 1973

Copyright © 1972 by
Ecumenical Foundation of America
Los Angeles, California
Library of Congress Catalog Card Number 74-187358
Lithographed in the United States by
Anderson, Ritchie & Simon
Los Angeles, California
Designed by Joseph Simon
and Cas Duchow

Table of Contents

Meditations on the Mount of Olives

The dream of every Christian is to undertake

a pilgrimage to Jerusalem; to climb the steep road to Golgotha

and there to relive the Passion of Christ,

where almost two thousand

years ago the hammer strokes on the Cross started

Christian civilization. Woe to Western man if these strokes

do not resound in his ears anymore.

—✧—

AUTHOR

Preface

During my trip around the world in 1961, I visited the Holy Land. For some fifteen days I settled on the Mount of Olives at *Dominus flevit*, where Our Lord lamented over Jerusalem. Each morning I descended for Mass to the Church of All Nations built on the Rock of Agony in the Gethsemane. Those pilgrim days were spent in prayer, meditation and reading the Bible. I turned the page of the fortieth year in my life.

One afternoon as I read the lives of the famous pilgrims, I suddenly became aware of "a beautiful princess from the far North . . . the richest woman of all Sweden . . . the mother of eight children . . . a widow, who in her fortieth year dedicated her life to Christ: Saint Birgitta."

I asked one of the friars about Saint Birgitta. In his singing Neapolitan dialect he recited, "If I had not already created the world, I would have created it now for you, Birgitta." Christ's words from the Franciscan devotions left a deep impression on me. In Naples I visited the baroque Church of Saint Birgitta, and in Rome I admired with a great sentiment the beautiful *Domus Birgittae*, where she lived for almost twenty-five years and died. Here Birgitta wrote her book of *Heavenly Revelations* about which Pope Boniface IX said, "they are inspired by the prophetic spirit." Emperor Maximilian the First preferred one illustrated edition of the *Revelations* to all his marble palaces. At the Vatican Library I familiarized myself with classic volumes of Burlamacchi, Flavigny and Jørgensen.

The saints are God's heroes. Their souls are the battlefields which reflect the agonies and ecstasies of every individual and his society. The twentieth century—already burdened with two World Wars and two major revolutions, "overpopulation," hunger and pestilence, and now problems of air, water and food poisoning—through a cumulative effect could face the death of civilization. The irreligious movements, family disintegration, drugs and alcoholism; film, theater and art perversions are causing the pollution of the soul bordering on suicide. I am sorry every time a tree is cut into pulp for pornographic literature. Indeed our time cries out for new saints.

Then I realized that the fourteenth century of Saint Birgitta was a very similar epoch of uncertainties and change. The Hundred Years' War raged between England and France, and gunpowder decimated the feudal armies. The Papacy moved from Rome to Avignon, heralding the Schism within the Church. The Turks were invading the Byzantine Empire, and the Western powers stood unprepared. The Black Death harvested almost half of Europe, causing labor shortages, peasant revolts and other social ills. As always during a time of change, immorality is at home. And just at this hour of darkness Providence chose a woman to descend from the far North into the heart of Christendom: Saint Birgitta of Sweden. Through her *Revelations* she fought a heroic battle to preserve and reform the Church and Christian civilization. Her prophecies and positions taken on slavery, property, government, celibacy, abortion, witchcraft and morals are classic.

Birgitta cleared the road for a new breed of men like the ecumenical Pope Eugene IV, Columbus, Sir Thomas More, Dürer, Erasmus, Michelangelo, Ignatius Loyola and Pope Paul III, who all fought the spiritual battles and saved Europe. The same process of renewal—again very much in the spirit of Saint Birgitta—was repeated in the seventeenth and nineteenth centuries. Prospects for the materialistic and secularistic twentieth century are indeed bleak, but again through heroic women like Birgitta who would ennoble womanhood, and men of vision who would recapture the lost horizons and if necessary seal their beliefs with the blood of the martyrs, the twenty-first century could be a Century of Faith.

The atomic age leaves little room for new heroes. But even in this computerized era the soul in its mystical way will always search for God. In fact the great pressures of our time could activate an individual soul just as extremely high pressure on carbon transforms it into a diamond. Birgitta was such a hard and shining diamond in her century; her name even means "hard, bright and exalted." It is not difficult to foresee that in the twenty-first century only people of strong faith will survive.

Toynbee postulates that societies rise and fall with the quality of their leadership. Recently Alvin Toffler has written, "Today as never before we need a multiplicity of visions, dreams and prophecies— images of potential tomorrow," in order to avoid the "future shock" and breakdown of society. And Teilhard de Chardin, referring to the next century, suggests that we "destroy the Grand Illusion by asceticism and by mysticism." Reading these great authors, one imagines he is reading Saint Birgitta's *Revelations*.

It is indeed a Grand Illusion to believe that one war can be ended with another war; that one revolution will be solved by a new cycle of revolutions; that drug abuse will be eliminated by putting more money into rehabilitation programs; or that crime will be conquered with more jails until half of humanity finds itself behind bars. All these problems are just shadows—Grand Illusions—of a deeper cause, and the solutions now being offered are just surface remedies. The issue is fundamental, at least in the framework of our Judeo-Christian civilization: through aberrations, wrongdoings and sin man has unbalanced the divine order of nature, of the universe and actually of his own psyche. Only by returning to God in love, humility and repentance can man solve this maze of problems and re-establish the balance between himself and his Creator. Heroic souls and leadership like Saint Birgitta's will show the way.

The results of all my endeavors are three volumes: *Anima Eroica*, a biography; *Iconography*, a pictorial expansion of Birgitta's life and work; and now *Revelations*, a review of her most important visions, prophecies and devotions. All three volumes have been published by the Ecumenical Foundation of America, established on Saint Birgitta's ideals of striving for Christian unity. And so ten years after my pilgrimage to the Holy Land the *Trilogy of Saint Birgitta* is complete. Through Birgitta I was reassured that "regardless of changes in history, God is never dead nor will He ever be."

I would like to express my deep gratitude to the Swedish scholars Andreas Lindblom, Professor Henrik Cornell, Sven Stolpe and Doctor Hans Cnattingius for their advice; grateful acknowledgment to the Vatican Library, Stockholm Royal Library, London University Library, Vienna University Library, Amsterdam University Library, Brussels University Library, Copenhagen University Library, Sorbonne University Library, Toronto University Library, Stanford University Library, University of California Library, University of Southern California Library, Loyola University Library, Munich State Library, Naples National Library, New York City Library and Los Angeles County Library; thankful appreciation to the Vatican Pinacoteca, Louvre in Paris, Prado in Madrid, Academy and Uffizi in Florence, National Museum in Nuremberg, Art Museum in Colmar, and to all churches involved in this project. The art reproductions of the Nativity and the Passion of Christ, as explained in the Chapters III and IV, are of transcendental importance.

A special recognition to Professor Carlo Pedretti of the University of California in Los Angeles, whose recent research into the religious art of Leonardo da Vinci established Saint Birgitta's *Revelations* as a source of inspiration. May the second edition of this volume inspire the students of art, history and theology for generations to come.

ANTHONY BUTKOVICH

Los Angeles, July 23, 1973

Chapter I

SIBYL OF THE NORTH

Sibyl of the North

There is a legend that a parish priest of Åbo had a vision of Our Lady seated with a book above the clouds: "A daughter has been born to Sir Birger, and her wondrous voice will be heard all over the world." To Sir Birger and Lady Ingeborg Persson the seventh child was born. As the wind blew over the mounds of the pagan gods and kings, Sir Birger could see the spires of the new Gothic cathedral on the horizon. The granite rock of Mora, where the kings were elected and crowned, was not far from his castle. The cathedral was close to Sir Birger's heart, and he stood in the midst of Swedish politics. Could he have any forebodings about the child just born? Only God in His wisdom knew that to the Perssons in the castle of Finsta in 1303 the Sibyl of the North was born.

Sir Birger was a lawmaker. Under him the Uppland law was rewritten, codified and promulgated as a national law to replace the pagan custom law. The new law was based on the Christian principle, "If people would follow the teaching of Christ, no laws would be necessary." Property was considered a lease from God, not an unlimited right as taught by Roman law. In medieval Sweden the Persson family was one of the most powerful. Through their children Sir Israel and Birgitta, the Perssons became related to several most influential families such as Sparre, Sture, Bielke, Bonde, Brahe and Vasa. Sture was a regent, Bonde an elected king, and Vasa a founder of a new royal dynasty. For two hundred and fifty years Sweden was under the influence of Birgitta's family.

Birgitta was raised by parents who did not dispute but lived by the Gospel. One snowy evening the eleven-year-old girl attended a sermon on the Passion of Christ. The preaching of a famous Dominican friar left a deep impression on her. The same evening as she prayed before the Crucifix, suddenly the room was filled with an ineffable light, and Christ appeared to Birgitta pointing to His five wounds. Only slowly she could utter, "Oh, my dearest Lord, who has ill-treated You so?" And Christ sadly answered, "All they who forgot Me and despise My love." At this moment Birgitta felt as if a gryphon's beak plunged into her heart. That moment which skeptics dispute so much and the saints pray for, had happened. Birgitta was in a state of grace. Fervently she recited the prayer which was to mean so much to the persecuted Christians in sixteenth-century Europe: "O Lord God, forgive me my sins for the sake of Thy bitter pain and for Thy love of the race of man. O Lord Jesus, Who was taken captive by enemies, have mercy upon me. O Lord Jesus, Who stoodest bound to the stake, have mercy upon me. O Lord Jesus, Who was without guilt and was judged by heartless men, have mercy upon me. O Lord Jesus, Thou Who was robbed of Thy garments, and clad in the raiment of mockery, have mercy upon me. O Lord Jesus, Who was so cruelly torn that Thy bones could be seen and there was not a whole spot upon Thee, have mercy upon me. O Lord Jesus, Thou Who was stretched upon the Cross, as a bird of prey is stretched with nails upon the door of a barn, have mercy upon me." The comparison to a bird of prey has its mystical meaning, referring to Christ as a gryphon who chooses only the finest hearts. That night Birgitta's was chosen.

Education was essential for Birgitta. Matthias of Linköping, a leading theologian of Sweden, taught her the rudiments of theology, philosophy and Church history. But it was Birgitta who advised Matthias to translate the Bible into Swedish. Bishop Niels Hermansson tutored her in the Latin language. Her crowning education came later in Rome from Bishop Alphonse of Jaen. Among the volumes which influenced Birgitta most were the *Lives of the Saints, Book of Chivalry* and Saint Bernard's *Liber de Modo Bene Vivendi*, which in its prologue outlines, "This book is a mirror in which the soul can see its stains and learn what is pleasing to God and what displeases Him. Read this book again and again, and you will learn how you must love God and your neighbor, despise what is earthly and transient, striving after the everlasting and heavenly, enduring for Christ's sake the adversities of this world and despising its prosperity and enticements, thanking God in sickness, not taking pride in good health, not becoming presumptuous in good fortune nor downcast in trials." Birgitta followed the footsteps of her favored Saint Bernard.

Although Birgitta preferred the convent to marriage, she obediently followed the will of her parents. At fourteen she married Prince Ulf Gudmarsson of Nericia. Realizing that a good marriage can lead to heaven, she later mused philosophically, "Virginity merits the crown, widowhood draws near to God, matrimony does not exclude one from heaven." Birgitta was the mother of eight children; best known among them were Saint Catherine and the chivalric Sir Charles, who was to cause his mother so much pain. About Birgitta's active life Catherine testified in the Process of Canonization: "Mother took me and my sisters with her to the hospital which she built, and without disgust she bound the wounds and sores with her own hands . . . and when mother was reproached for taking her little girls with her, that we might be infected from the stench of the sick people, she answered that she took us while we were still small, so that we might learn at an early age to serve God and His poor and sick . . . and already, while father was still living, and later when mother was a widow, she did not sit down at the table without having given twelve poor people food to eat, and every Friday she washed their feet herself. Each year mother sent clothes to the poor and alms to the many convents around the country." It is true Birgitta was one of the richest women of Sweden, but she did not believe only in mercy and charity, but in a social Christianity based on justice, where the Kingdom of God is also on earth. Catholic Action by Pope Pius XI was based on these principles. To remain forever reminded Pius XI kept a portrait of Saint Birgitta on his working desk.

King Magnus Eriksson married Blanche of Namur, and his cousin Birgitta joined the court of Stockholm. To Blanche the petite and blonde Birgitta appeared like a fairy-tale princess. Blanche could not suspect that under the heavy brocade and jewels was a rough penitent shirt or those azure eyes beheld the Crucifix during many hours of daily prayer. In order to avoid the frivolous gossip of the court Birgitta chewed a bitter herb. The only happiness that Blanche brought to her was in the relics of saintly King Louis of France. To the last crusading king and model knight, the teaching of the Church and everyday Christian practice were the same. They were also the same with Birgitta, but not so with Magnus and Blanche. King Magnus replaced the old royal advisers with young flatterers. When the king was unable to pay his debt to Denmark for the province of Scania, Birgitta saw the Swedish hostages being taken into slavery. Saddened, she and her husband Prince Ulf left on a pilgrimage.

Birgitta embarked for her first pilgrimage to the shrine of Saint Olaf of Norway at Trondheim. King Olaf carried the Gospel to heathens and met a martyr's death in the battle of Stiklastadt in 1030. The pilgrims took thirty-five days to march over the snowy mountains. Pilgrimages to the shrines of the Apostles and saints in the Middle Ages were spiritual exercises in endurance, and it was not Birgitta, but her husband Ulf, who tired. At the tomb of Saint Olaf she prayed for the wretched court of King Magnus. Then, for love of God and her country she returned to Stockholm.

Birgitta found the court even more frivolous than before. King Magnus and Blanche were under the influence of a Doctor von Wampen and his book *The Mirror of Nature*, in which he expounded the arts of pleasure: "Enjoy the pleasure of love-making until you die, for you do not know how long you will live to do it still." A courtier, Bengt Algotsson, whom men and women found equally attractive, had a firm grip over King Magnus and Blanche. Birgitta's spiritual eyes could perceive the threat of sin at work. "Three devils rule in this land: the

5

first is drunkenness, the second voluptuousness and the third unnatural intercourse." (Rev. VI. 80) Higher Court expenditures led to higher taxes and oppression, and they in turn resulted in revolts and ill-fated war with Russia. To combat the worldliness of the court and Sweden, Christ appeared to Birgitta commanding her to found a new national monastery of nuns and monks in Vadstena, the monastery to be in honor of the Mother of God. As Johannes Jørgensen in his classic work writes, "Birgitta would create a new army of warriors of God and gather them to fight under a banner as red as blood, bearing a picture of the Cross of Christ." And then Christ, after dictating to her the rules of the new Order of the Holy Saviour, proceeded: "Read the Rule and speak to the Pope about this Rule which I dictated with My own lips." (Rev. VIII. 51) But that would mean first to bring the Pope back to Rome from Avignon. To cleanse herself again from the odor of the Swedish court Birgitta undertook an arduous pilgrimage to Saint James of Compostella.

Before leaving Sweden, Birgitta visited the shrine of Saint Botvid. The martyred saint revealed to her, "I and other saints have gained for you the grace of God that you shall see and hear the spiritual meanings, and the spirit of God shall inflame your soul." (Extrav. 72) The road took Prince Ulf and Birgitta through Lübeck where some hundred and fifty years later the first master edition of the *Book of Revelations* was to be published. In Cologne they stopped at the tombs of the Three Kings. Because of the Hundred Years' War the pilgrims avoided Paris and left from Marseilles to Spain. At Compostella, Birgitta was deeply impressed by the Knights of Saint James; it was there she probably conceived her idea of a spiritual and military knighthood, knights with a vow of a monk's chastity and with a soldier's obedience. In iconography Saint James and Saint Birgitta are the only saints portrayed as pilgrims.

Returning home on the Road of the Kings, where so many saints and kings walked on pilgrimages through the centuries, Birgitta stopped in Fontaine, the birthplace of her favored Saint Bernard. In

Arras, where centuries later a Birgittine convent was to be built and some nuns were to find a martyr's death during the French Revolution, her husband Ulf took on fever. Birgitta had a vision of the patron Saint Dionysius of France: "I am Dionysius, who came from Rome to this part of France to preach the word of God. And because you have always had a devotion to me, I have taken you under my protection. And I say to you that you will come to Rome and Jerusalem, and by you God will be made known to the world. And I will always help you and stand by you, and this will be a proof to you, that your husband shall not die of this sickness." (Extrav. 92) Prince Ulf survived, and on returning to Sweden he entered the monastery of Alvastra as he had vowed. At peace with God and himself he died a few months later. Birgitta, in the grand tradition of a Catholic widow, found herself in the silence of the monastery where she prayed, contemplated and bound her will to God's through penitence.

Birgitta did not climb the mountain of mystical experience as most saints do, for she was already under the grace of God. Christ again appeared to her: "I am speaking not only to you but to all Christians. You will be My bride; you will see and hear the spiritual truths and penetrate into the celestial secrets, and My spirit will dwell in you until your death." (Extrav. 47) At this moment Birgitta felt a movement under her heart as if she had conceived — a mystical experience about which Saint Catherine of Siena and Saint Therese of Avila wrote so much. She felt like the heroines in the Old Testament, for "her heart was warm and in her thoughts a burning fire." Stoically Birgitta took her wedding ring off. "When I buried my husband I buried all my earthly love with him, for though I loved him as my own soul, I would not for a penny buy back his life against the will of God. As long as I kept this wedding ring it was like a burden to me, because I remembered my lost joy. But now my soul will love God only, and therefore I will forget both my ring and my husband." (Extrav. 93) Prior Peter Olafsson knew as a theologian that the devil could not tempt Birgitta in her service to the greater glory of God. But Christ had His own way of throwing His servant into the battlefield; He ordered Birgitta to return to the court. "I am happy to obey what is commanded to me for love of Him Who obeyed His Father unto death." (Rev. VI. 49)

After her spiritual life at Alvastra her whole being revolted against the frivolity of the court. It took all the strength of her spirit to return to King Magnus as an adviser. This time she no longer dressed in heavy brocades and jewels, but in the black robes of a widow, her face pale and beautified through silent suffering and her only adornment a chain with a Cross. In apocalyptic language she warned the leaders of the country to repent, for the Day of Judgment was near. Her brother, Sir Israel, who as a member of the royal council knew the truth about the state of affairs in the kingdom, stood faithfully by Birgitta. But her own son Sir Charles went along with the court life, which brought Birgitta into a biblical anger. King Magnus and the Queen were impressed with their saintly cousin. The king lessened the tax burden to please her and to make himself popular. He bestowed some lands and buildings for the national monastery at Vadstena.

Birgitta was also interested in saving individual souls at the time of oncoming Judgment. A handsome knight, Sir Magnus d'Eka, although married, favored the court's easy morals. Christ once again spoke through Birgitta, and it took one conversation to persuade Sir Magnus to repent. He became her devout knight and later, when a widower, joined the priesthood. Birgitta's fame spread through the capital when a notorious courtesan repented her way of life. Like Mary Magdalen repenting to Christ, she was morally resurrected. Later she claimed that a holy flame blazed from Birgitta. Some two hundred miracles are recorded of her healing, her bringing people to repentance and exorcizing the devil out of sinners and those possessed.

Powerful courtiers became envious and worked against Birgitta's influence over the king. A scandal broke out when King Magnus followed Birgitta's advice and dismissed a tax collector for his dishonesty. Even the bishops were divided on Birgitta; five of them defended her, whereas two worldly ones turned against her. Birgitta had a great love for the priesthood, and she often commented, "Neither angels nor prophets can do what a priest has the privilege to do — administer the Sacraments." But when it came to the morals or celibacy of the priests, Birgitta proved to be uncompromising.

King Magnus pretended to follow the advice of Birgitta, but kept a secret council with his favorite Bengt Algotsson. During the day the king would run around the court in a penitent garb, with his Bible in his hand, but at night he would masquerade as a woman and make merry. King Magnus' double standard — his being divided against himself — was to be his final downfall. But still he was shrewd enough to use Birgitta's moral authority in blessing the Crusade against the Russians. In vain Birgitta warned the king that the Crusade must be undertaken in good faith and that the conversion of the heathens in Finland, Estonia and Livonia must be made with the Cross and not with the sword alone.

King Magnus did not know that Christ revealed to Birgitta, "The time will come when the heathens will become so pious that the Christians will be like their humble servants, and the Holy Scriptures will be fulfilled, in saying that there shall be one flock and One Shepherd, one faith and one clear knowledge of God. Then many who were called shall be rejected, but the wilderness shall blossom, and the heathens shall sing, 'Glory be to the Father and to the Son and to the Holy Ghost.' " (Rev. VI. 77) But King Magnus had hidden motives behind the Crusade: to rid himself of some powerful lords and to replenish his empty treasury with the plunder of war. He consulted a sorceress who falsely predicted a Swedish victory. Some Norwegian and Swedish knights did fight for the Cross in the spirit of Birgitta, but most of them were foreign mercenaries who had only looting, rape and murder in mind. King Magnus, although he initially won the fortress of Nøteborg, lost the war against the Russians. After losing the war and bankrupting the country, the court entered into a post-deluge mood. "But now men and women are sinning in the kingdom of Sweden, and most of all those who are of the class of courtiers and knights, as the devil once sinned. For they pride themselves in their beautiful bodies which I have given them. They strive after riches which I have not willed to give them. Thus they fall into hideous desires, and if it were possible they would rather kill Me than renounce their concupiscence, and they pay no heed to the terrible Judgment which will come upon them for their sins. The beautiful bodies in which they take pride shall be torn asunder and devoured by wild birds and animals. The possessions which they have gathered against My will shall be seized by others and they themselves shall hunger. Because of their abominable concupiscence they displease My Father so much that He will never find them worthy to behold His countenance. And because, if they could, they would surely kill Me, they shall be given into the hands of the devil and they shall be slain by him in hell with an everlasting death." (Processus p. 632) Then Birgitta stepped forward with the voice of Christ: "I shall visit this kingdom with a sword and lance and with wrath . . . I shall rise up in all My power and will not spare young or old, rich or poor, just or unjust. I shall come with My plough and pull up the trees by the roots, so that from a thousand people only a hundred will be left, and their homes shall stand empty." (Extrav. 74) The Black Death struck all over Scandinavia; Sweden was decimated as *Diarium Vazstenense* of the year 1350 states, ". . . at that time a great mortality prevailed in Sweden, greater than any could remember to have been before or since, which Birgitta had foretold long before would come." King Magnus in a penitent garb with a heavy Cross around his neck called on people from town to town to repent as Birgitta always urged him. But her voice was not to be heard anymore in Sweden. As an obedient bride of Christ she followed His command: "Go to Rome . . . and stay in Rome until you see the Pope and Emperor together, and then you will proclaim My words to them." (Extrav. 8) The road led her from Kalmar, Stralsund, Lübeck, Cologne, Altomünster, Bergamo, Milano, Genoa for eternal Rome. Birgitta's apostolate was about to begin.

Chapter II

THE AMBASSADRESS OF GOD

The Ambassadress of God

Birgitta reached Italy. At the tomb of Saint Ambrose in Milano it was revealed to her, "Because of the prayers of your friends, God has called upon you so that you may in spirit see and hear and understand, and what you have thus heard in spirit you will reveal to others." (Rev. III. 5) She paid a visit to the haughty Archbishop Giovanni Visconti, who neglected his archbishopric, waging war against Pope Clement VI. Visconti must have marveled at the courageous woman reproaching him for his absenteeism. Pope Clement VI excommunicated him. Centuries later at the Council of Trent, Archbishop Charles Borromeo of Milano was to call for reforms against absenteeism.

The dream of every medieval Christian was to make a pilgrimage to Rome, then a city of pagan ruins and medieval towers, lonely monasteries and shattered churches. Two years before Birgitta's arrival an earthquake and fire had partially destroyed Saint Peter's Basilica. But her mind did not dwell over the Roman ruins; all that interested her was the ruin of the Church. Rome did not have more than fifty thousand inhabitants, and the Church less than one thousand priests, monks and nuns. As Birgitta exclaimed, "Rome sits like a sorrowing widow longing for her bridegroom." The Pope was being held in Avignon in so-called Babylonian captivity.

Several years earlier Birgitta had sent her envoys Bishop Hemming and the Prior Peter Olafsson to Pope Clement VI with a revelation: "Do your utmost to establish peace between the kings of England and France, who are fighting each other like wild animals and traitors to their souls. Then come to Italy and proclaim the Holy Year." (Rev. VI. 63) Birgitta was aware of the Hundred Years' War during her pilgrimage through France. Now in Rome she could hear the lamentations of the pilgrims about the ravages of war. The Pope in Avignon did not escape the looting and killing of the marauding armies. At the battle of Crécy and Poitiers the French chivalry was massacred. To Birgitta this war between the cousins King Edward III and King Phillip VI of Valois was a fratricidal war: "They are like two wild beasts. One of them is greedy to swallow everything it can; the more it eats the hungrier it gets, and its hunger is never satisfied. The other wants to exalt itself above all men and rule over them. Each of the two animals tries to swallow the heart of the other. Their terrible voices are heard far and wide across the world, and their cries are this: 'Take the gold and riches of the world, and do not spare the blood of Christian men.' " (Rev. IV. 104) King Edward III, Richard II and his sons met violent deaths, and after the battle of Agincourt King Henry V married the French princess, as Birgitta prophesied. If it hadn't been for the appearance of Joan of Arc, the marriage might have established peace between England and France.

In the year 1350, Pope Clement VI proclaimed the Jubilee. Regardless of the Hundred Years' War and the Black Death more than a million pilgrims descended on Rome. Over the hills and ruins where sheep roamed freely during the day, brigands lurked at night. Many pilgrims were robbed, raped and murdered. Papal vicar Ponzio Perotti opened La Porta Sacra of Saint Peter's and the ceremonies exalted the medieval souls. But to lodge and feed all the pilgrims became difficult, so the papal legate Cardinal Anibale Gaetani limited each pilgrim's stay to a few days. Romans interested in business and pilgrims interested in their souls rioted; the legate put Rome under interdict and escaped to Naples. Birgitta warned both the vicar and the legate to care less for the coffers of gold and silver of Avignon and more for the souls of pilgrims: "You should know that a great thunder and lightning will strike the Church. The fall of the Church will be so great that all of Christendom will be shaken." (Rev. IV. 78) The Sibyl sitting among the ruins of Rome foresaw the Schism when there would be two or three popes at the same time. Pope Urban VI was to cite Birgitta's revelation against the antipope Clement VII.

Birgitta lamented over Rome as an Old Testament prophetess over Jerusalem: "In times past the city was dyed purple with the blood of martyrs and built upon the bones of saints. Now her gates have been thrown down and are lying on the ground, her altars are desolate, her walls without watchmen. Oh Rome, if thou knewest the day of thy visitation, thou wouldst weep and not rejoice. Oh Rome, Rome, be converted and turn to the Lord thy God." (Rev. III. 27) Some ecclesiasts smiled about Birgitta's religious zeal. Her warning of a new visitation reminded others of the Gothic sacking of Rome. But to her devout followers Birgitta's was truly the voice of God.

Birgitta stayed at the hostel of Ursi facing the castle San Angelo. When Cardinal Hugo de Beaufort learned of the distinguished pilgrim, he offered her the palace adjacent to Saint Lorenzo in Damasso. The palace was situated in the domain of the Orsini family between Saint Peter's and Campo di Fiori. The Colonna family occupied the area between the Colosseum and the Lateran Basilica. Birgitta devoted her time to visiting the seven pilgrim churches and to attending the hospitals with her daughter Catherine, who had arrived in the meantime from Sweden. The only social contact Birgitta cherished was her friendship with the Orsinis, who gave her insight into the political and cultural trends in Italy. Bishop Alphonse of Jaen abandoned a rich bishopric to become her confessor.

The Holy Year ended when civil disorders broke out between the powerful families of Orsini, Colonna, Savelli and Frangipani. As always when anarchy prevails, a dictator readily appears on the stage of history, this time in the person of Cola di Rienzi, mystic and humanist, visionary and political revolutionary. Both Pope Clement VI and his far-sighted Cardinal-soldier Egidius Albornoz understood that Rienzi could serve as a scourge for the troublesome lords. Indeed reminiscent of the past glory of Rome, Rienzi marched on the Capitol and was acclaimed by the people. He humiliated the Orsinis and Colonnas by imprisoning them. Now they preferred the Pope to the upstart dictator Rienzi. When Rienzi levied taxes on salt and wine, a sore wound for the Romans, they rioted, overthrew and murdered him. Albornoz with his masterful policy unified the Papal State and proclaimed a new constitution which lasted until the nineteenth century. This Spanish Cardinal-soldier greatly admired Birgitta of Sweden.

During Rienzi's tumults and disorders Birgitta almost became a victim of the anti-Orsini crowds which stormed her palace. Ever since Birgitta miraculously healed Prince Latino Orsini, she had become a close friend of the Orsini family. As Prior Peter Olafsson wrote, "During the first fifteen years when the bride of Christ was in Rome awaiting the coming of the Pope and Emperor, she received and published many revelations. She complained about the moral conditions in Rome, the sin and vicissitudes, and she threatened the Romans with severe punishments. Some Romans became inflamed with a deadly enmity, and some claimed that she might be sorceress who should be burned as a witch." (Process of Canonization) However, Birgitta did not stop warning the Romans: "And now I must speak to Rome like the prophets of Jerusalem. In former times justice dwelt in the city; its chiefs were princes of peace, but now they have become slayers of men." (Rev. III. 26) But Christ comforted Birgitta not to fear, and like a true Viking she stood her ground until the storm subsided. Her friendship with the Orsinis was expanded by another Orsini family in Naples. From then on the Orsinis served as her ambassadors.

Upon her arrival in Rome, Birgitta had first visited Saint Peter's Basilica, where at the tomb of the Apostle she received a revelation: "I tell you that you will live long enough to see with your own eyes My Vicegerent come back to Rome, and you will hear the people: 'Long live the Pope.' " (Rev. IV. 15) Indeed this prophecy was fulfilled when Pope Urban V arrived at Corneto on June 3, 1367 greeted by the jubilation of the Italians. Many reasons prompted the Pope to leave France. The Black Death had ravished Avignon; mercenaries had pillaged

Provence; the Turks were approaching Europe. Cardinal Albornoz had pacified Italy, and Emperor Charles IV, approving the rights and privileges of the Papal State, agreed to enter Rome accompanying the Pope. The next year the Emperor and Count Amadeus of Savoy escorted Pope Urban V from the Basilica Santa Maria Maggiore to Saint Peter's. The revelation already received in Sweden, "Go to Rome . . . and stay in Rome until you see the Pope and Emperor together, and then you will proclaim My words to them," was ready to be fulfilled. For the first time in a hundred and fifty years the Pope and the Emperor met again in Rome. Now was the time, Birgitta knew, to obtain the confirmation of her Religious Order of the Holy Saviour.

Emperor Charles IV was aware of Birgitta's revelation, "To the Emperor of Germany . . . receive the Rule, which I have dictated to the woman who is writing to you . . . read the Rule, and see to it that what I have approved before the face of My heavenly host is also confirmed by My vicar on earth." (Rev. VIII. 51) Together with the Bible, Birgitta's *Revelations* were the Emperor's favorite reading, and they were studied at the universities of Prague and Bratislava.

Prince Latino Orsini, now a commander in chief of the Papal forces, arranged the audience for Birgitta through his friend Cardinal Pierre Roger de Beaufort. Birgitta was escorted by Bishop Alphonse, Prince Niccolò Orsini and General Gomez Albornoz. The nephew of the great Cardinal Albornoz also became a devoted follower of Birgitta. The audience took place at the Pope's summer residence in Montefiascone overlooking the lake of Bolsena. Since the Lateran Council of 1215, all new orders accepted either the Rule of Saint Augustine or Saint Benedict. Even Saint Dominic obeyed this provision. It was arranged that the Constitution of the Order of the Holy Saviour would serve as a supplement to the Rule of Saint Augustine. Birgitta, although disappointed, graciously accepted.

The Emperor of the Eastern Roman Empire, John V Paleologus, arrived to pay homage to Pope Urban V. Paleologus, endangered from the Turks, expected a united Christendom to undertake a Crusade. King Edward III and Charles V of France were too busy with the Hundred Years' War and disregarded the plea. Emperor Charles IV was also unable to aid Paleologus, for his hands were tied by the provision of the Golden Bull. Times had indeed changed: Charles IV could no more compare with Charlemagne than Paleologus with Justinian. Only the exterior imperial symbols and trappings were preserved. Birgitta anticipated the downfall of Byzantium: "Those Greeks who know that there is only one Christian faith, that is, Catholic, and only one Vicegerent of Christianity, namely the Bishop of Rome, yet who will not obey him as their rightful shepherd, will after death find no mercy with God. It is different with those who have never come into knowledge of the Catholic Church, and who live a good and pious life according to the best dictates of their consciences — upon them God will have mercy. For the rest, the Greeks must understand that the whole of their Kingdom is at the point of falling, and that the Byzantine Empire will perish before long." (Rev. VII. 19) The Turks conquered Constantinople, and the Eastern Roman Empire was brought to an end in 1453.

Following the advice of numerous French Cardinals, Pope Urban V decided to leave Rome. The Italians were dismayed, the Frenchmen jubilant. Beyond the veil of human emotions Birgitta could sense the impending tragedy. Our Lady revealed to her, "I will speak to you of the Pope whose name is Urban. To him the Holy Spirit gave the counsel that he should come to Rome to work justice and strengthen the Christian faith and renew the Holy Church. And as a mother leads her child whither she will, by showing him her breasts, so I led him to Rome by my prayers. What does he now do? He turns his back on me, and not his face, and would leave me. And a false and evil spirit would entice him to do this. For it wearies him to do his duty, and he is longing for ease and comfort. He is longing for his own country, and his carnally minded friends urge him to depart, for they think more of his temporal welfare and conform more to his will than to the will of God and to what serves the glory of God and the everlasting good of the Pope. If he should succeed in getting back to his own country, he will be struck such a blow that his teeth will shake in his mouth, his sight will be darkened and all his limbs will tremble . . . The friends of God will no longer include him in their prayers, and he will be called to account to God for what he did and what he did not do." (Rev. IV. 38) Birgitta, already an old woman, climbed one of the steepest hills in Italy at Montefiascone to warn the Pope. Cardinal Pierre Roger de Beaufort did not dare deliver the message to Pope Urban V, as Bishop Alphonse writes, "And though she might well be afraid to speak so boldly to so great a lord, she feared neither death nor any peril." Urban V left Italy accompanied by the tears of the faithful and had hardly put his foot on the soil of Avignon when he was struck by fever. Remembering Birgitta's revelation, he had himself carried down to the garden cottage in his simple Benedictine garb so that all visitors could see "how the glory of this world passes into ashes." He died repentant to Birgitta, but as Petrarca wrote, " among the sinners of Avignon." The tremor of the fulfillment of Birgitta's prophecy reached the farthest corner of the Christian world. Cardinal Pierre Roger de Beaufort, a friend of Birgitta, was elected Pope Gregory XI. The Avignon papacy was nearing its end.

Though Birgitta lived in Rome, she was well-informed about the situation in Sweden. On Christmas, 1369, her sons Sir Charles and Sir Birger arrived in Rome after twenty years of absence. They gave her a full report: King Magnus had lost a Crusade against the Russians, further bankrupting the country. His favorite Bengt Algotsson wrongly advised him to abandon his allies, the Hansa League and the Teutonic Order. Yet Algotsson was promoted to Duke of Finland, to the dismay of the whole country. Pope Innocent VI excommunicated King Magnus for not repaying his loan and for his additional taxation of Church properties. The seeds of future trouble that would lead Gustav Vasa into the Reformation were sown.

Birgitta believed in the natural frontiers of Sweden, not in man-made ones. She had warned, "The Lord declared to Magnus that if he abandons one part of his kingdom, he will lose his power and finish his career in shame and prison." (Rev. IV. 3) Indeed King Magnus lost the rich province of Scania to King Valdemar of Denmark. Birgitta wrote a famous letter to the royal council advising it to depose Magnus as a tyrant responsible for damaging the moral and material interests of Sweden. After the strange death of the young heir, Duke Erik, and his wife, civil war broke out. King Magnus was then deposed, imprisoned and exiled to Norway where he accidentally drowned. His favorite Bengt Algotsson was murdered by the relatives. So ended the personal glory of two men who brought Sweden into ruin. Then Prince Albrecht of Mecklenburg, or "the fox," as Birgitta referred to him, was elected to the throne of Sweden. The *Folkungsaga* had come to a sad end, as Birgitta had prophesied a long time before.

Birgitta left Rome for a pilgrimage to the South, visiting the tombs of the Apostles Saint Andrew in Amalfi, Saint Bartholomew in Benevento and Saint Matthew in Salerno. Strengthened by the voices of these Apostles, she entered the city of Naples, an enchanting city situated under the slopes of Vesuvius, embraced by vineyards and orchards and facing the profile of Capri. The Greeks and Romans, Moslems and Normans, Germans and Spaniards, Frenchmen and Hungarians, Albanians and Dalmatians, all had embroidered the tapestry of Naples, the city where Saint Thomas Aquinas wrote his *Summa* and Boccaccio his *Decameron*.

When Birgitta with her retinue of pilgrims arrived in Naples, Queen Giovanna, deeply impressed with the saintly prophetess, arranged a royal reception in her honor. Birgitta's handsome son Sir Charles, instead of kissing the brocade shoe of the queen as court protocol required, kissed her lips. This spark of passion did not escape the jealous courtiers nor Birgitta, who sensed a drama in the making. Queen Giovanna in full blossom of her womanhood resembled a heroine from Boccaccio's *Decameron*. For Sir Charles the bacchantic carnival days were only an intriguing interlude; the charming Swedish knight could not keep the rhythm of the passionate South and soon died of consumption of the lungs. The colorful carnival transfigured itself into a macabre funeral. Queen Giovanna and the Neapolitans were heartbroken, but not Birgitta, who loved her son most: "If I knew that he would become a king, I would not wish him back to *this* misery." For the Gothic Birgitta only sin was death. She forgave Queen Giovanna, presenting to her a golden Cross and asking her to pray for all sinners. And so Birgitta's prophecy to Prince Orsini in Rome, that "all will visit and return from the Holy Land except one," was fulfilled. To this day in Southern Italy there is a legend that eight days before a person is to die, Birgitta visits him and prepares him for a gentle death.

Queen Giovanna loved life with a Southern passion. She married her cousin King Andrew of Hungary, whom she poisoned to free herself for a more passionate cousin, Prince Louis of Taranto. After Louis died prematurely, she married "the handsomest man in the world," King James of Aragon, who preferred to stay alive far away in Majorca than to die prematurely in Naples. After Pope Urban V returned from Avignon, Giovanna paid him homage in Rome. However, when Urban VI was later elected Pope, she sided with the French antipope Clement VII. Apparently her French blood was stronger than her wisdom. Her fourth husband, Prince Otto von Brunswick, on his way to Giovanna was captured by Prince Charles of Durazzo who poisoned him. Queen Giovanna was later imprisoned and strangled by the avengers of her first husband King Andrew. The cycle was completed as Birgitta had prophesied.

Birgitta remained at Giovanna's court and left a deep impression on the assembly when she preached about Christian virtues: "Cleanse your bodies by a discreet abstinence which does not kill the flesh, but sin, and does not weaken but strengthen the spirit." At the court Birgitta met the cousin of the late Pope Urban V, Eleazar de Sabran, a young man who lived under the influence of Boccaccio. In him Birgitta could discern a calling for the priesthood. She explained to Eleazar that the excitement of all his youthful escapades was just an illusion, that luxuries enervate the flesh and weaken the will and that everyone must work toward his Salvation. Eleazar followed her motherly advice, and years later, when he became a great Cardinal, he took part in the canonization of Birgitta. Through the noble Lady Lapa Buondelmonti she met Niccolò Acciaiuoli, prime minister of the Kingdom of Naples, who brought Louis of Taranto into marriage with Queen Giovanna against the law of the Church. Acciaiuoli blamed himself, but he distributed his wealth to the Church and the poor and died repentant in the motherly arms of Birgitta. She assured his sister Lady Lapa that after purgatory he would see His Lord. However, Birgitta did not spare the society at court, reproaching them for many sins: "Many men and women run for advice and help to those accursed witches and sorceresses that they may have children, others to win love of man and woman, others to know what the future might bring or to be healed of their diseases. But all who do this or have dealings with such witcheries and sorceries, and all who harbor or shelter those who do this or trust in them, are hated and accursed in the sight of God." (Rev. VII. 29)

Another sin that Birgitta attacked was that committed against one's neighbor. She earned her popularity as a Christian heroine when she condemned those masters who kept slaves in Naples. The daughter of Sir Birger Persson, who in his Uppland law abolished slavery, "for when Christ was sold He redeemed all Christians," Birgitta considered it a scandal that slavery be permitted in a Christian country. As Johannes Jørgensen translated the Rev. VII. 30, "Here, in Naples, the Christians were no better than the infidels, in keeping female slaves like harlots, overburdening the male slaves with work, reviling and beating them so that in despair many committed suicide. These sins greatly angered God and the whole heavenly host, for God loves all human beings. He has created them all and has redeemed them all by His Passion on the Cross." Five hundred years later Abraham Lincoln echoed a similar biblical language.

When Birgitta returned from the Holy Land to Naples for the last time, she found the city engulfed in gloom and despair. The ravages of the Black Death had depleted and impoverished the population. Everyone then remembered the earlier warnings of Birgitta to repent or to face the Day of Judgment. This time Birgitta preferred to stay at the hospice of the Knights of Malta. Dressed in pilgrim's clothes, she faced Queen Giovanna, surrounded by her courtiers and courtesans in rich and enticing attires. With her biblical anger Birgitta thundered against the court's immodesty and sensuality in the midst of suffering and poverty: "But of surety they must know that so often as those women paint their faces, so often will the presence of the Holy Spirit be diminished in their souls. And so often as they dress in this immodest attire, so often will the beauty of their souls be lessened." (Rev. VII. 27) Knowing that pagan vices permeated the walls of Naples, Birgitta fiercely rebuked those women who were killing the foetus through abortion: "Some women behave like harlots; when they feel the life of a child in their wombs, they induce herbs or other means to cause miscarriage, only to perpetuate their amusement and unchastity. Therefore I shall deprive them from everlasting life and send them to everlasting death." (Rev. VII. 27) Many at the court repented and became devout followers of Birgitta.

A great devotee of Birgitta, Archbishop Bernardi of Naples, assembled all doctors and masters of theology and civic leaders to hear her in person. Christ spoke through Birgitta, who had just arrived from the Holy Land: "Princes of the world do not think now of undertaking pilgrimages to the places where I was born and suffered — instead they now prefer to go to races." (Rev. VII. 16) She spoke about the problems of the Church: "A Pope who would allow priests to marry will lose his spiritual vision and hearing and be robbed of all pious words and deeds; after death he will be cast into hell to be tormented forever and to become the food of devils through all eternity. And those priests who do not live in purity and continence of the flesh are accursed by God and worthy of losing their offices." (Rev. VII. 10) To Birgitta celibacy was a precious jewel shining brightly in the Catholic Church. The Archbishop read her revelations from the pulpit of the cathedral. Later he took part in the canonization of Saint Birgitta. To most Neapolitans Birgitta already was a saint; three churches already held her portraits.

Birgitta's apostolate in Naples reached its end. At the palace of Orsini in Naples she assured all those present that Pope Gregory XI would soon return. Young Roberto Orsini smiled in disbelief, but Birgitta assured him that he would accompany the Pope into Rome. The situation in Italy appeared hopeless. Everything the great Cardinal Albornoz had achieved in unifying the Papal State fell apart. The Viscontis once again behaved like the kings of Lombardy. Florence still remained propapal but turned its government into an oligarchy. Naples and Bologna, although actually papal dominions, were vacillating. The national spirit, awakened by Arnold of Brescia, Dante and Cola di Rienzi, moved like an underground tremor throughout Italy. The Avignon papacy ruled Italy through French legates, vicars and officials — to the dismay of the Italians.

Our Lady appeared to Birgitta with a revelation: "If Pope Gregory will come to Rome and return to Italy to stay and like a good shepherd take upon himself the cause of the Church . . . I will set his soul free from all earthly desire and worldly joy . . . for it is the will of God that he shall humbly bring back the Chair of Peter to Rome." (Rev. IV. 139) Birgitta, almost seventy years old, fought her last battle with the Pope: "If Pope Gregory does not come to Rome, everything that he now possesses in Italy shall be torn asunder and given to his enemies. And then he will never be able to regain it." (Rev. IV. 140) When Visconti convinced Venice and Florence to join the antipapal league, Pope Gregory, the spiritual child of the indomitable Birgitta, moved decisively. At great cost ten thousand Breton mercenaries were recruited, and they crossed the Alps to descend upon Florence. Trade was cut off, and the rich republic suffered great losses. The antipapal league faltered, and the head of Florence, Soderini, called upon Saint Catherine of Siena to intervene with the Pope to make peace. Soderini many years before had met Birgitta and her daughter in Naples and had named his two daughters after the Swedish saints. Bishop Alphonse of Jaen, himself half-Italian from Siena, served as an intermediary between Soderini, Catherine of Siena and the Pope. In September, 1376, Pope Gregory XI, escorted by twenty-two galleys of the Grand Master of the Order of Malta, left for Italy. At Ostia, Roberto

Orsini held the rein of the Pope's steed, remembering the words of Birgitta in Naples. On his finger he wore the ring of Birgitta, left to the Orsini family as a legacy. After seventy years the Avignon papacy had come to an end, and Birgitta could smile from heaven when her successor, Catherine of Siena, received Pope Gregory XI at Saint Peter's Basilica.

Since her pilgrimage to Golgotha, that ultimate dream of every Christian, Birgitta felt her earthly life coming to end. She returned to Rome and settled in her *Domus Birgittae*, a little palace bestowed upon her by the devout Countess Papazzuri, and began making arrangements for her departure. For the last time she visited the seven pilgrim churches of Rome. During these last days she envisioned centuries ahead: "I beheld from the Pope's palace in Rome to castle San Angelo and from that to the hospital of Santo Spirito and back again to Saint Peter's as if it were a wide plain, and the plain was surrounded by a very strong wall. And I heard a voice that said, 'The Pope who loves the Bride with the love of Christ and His holy friends shall live here with his counsellors and shall rule the Church of God in freedom and peace.'" (Rev. VI. 74) In 1870, Pope Pius IX, as a "prisoner of the Vatican," was reminded of this prophecy. When the Roman Question was settled through the Lateran Treaty in 1929, Pope Pius XI remembered "that little corner of earth" prophesied by Birgitta some six hundred years before.

The final concern of Birgitta was her monastery in Vadstena. She received from Christ her very last revelation reassuring her, "You shall not see all that you have written in the books of your *Heavenly Revelations* become reality, but for the sake of your good will you shall be counted a nun and abbess in Vadstena, and God will keep all His promises to you." (Extrav. 97) Her devout friends Orsini, Colonna, Savelli, Frangipani, Pignatelli and Ottaviani paid their last homage with sorrow. Birgitta received them with the gentle smile of a heroic woman who in her quest of the Holy Grail fought a good fight and found her Salvation. She advised her children Catherine and Sir Birger on the virtues of "silence and patience." Birgitta received the Holy

Communion, and with the whisper, "Into Your hands, O Lord, I commend my Spirit," the seventy-year-old ambassadress of God departed for her heavenly audience. The Roman sun seemed to stand still. It was July 23, 1373.

The death of the Angel of Rome, as Birgitta was affectionately known, covered the Eternal City with a veil of deep melancholy. The Romans were accustomed to receiving her revelations as a sort of special bulletins. From time to time the Romans had witnessed Birgitta's miracles in healing the sick, especially children, or driving demons out of the possessed. Now the people, along with the princes of Church and State, escorted her cortège by Via Flaminia out of the walls of Rome. The procession stopped at first in Montefiascone, where she once met Pope Urban V; then in Spoleto, where the governor, General Albornoz, paid tribute to his spiritual mother. From Ancona *via marem* to Trieste and then by carriage through Austria, Moravia, Poland and Prussia to the seaport of Danzig, Birgitta's procession continued on its way to the North. Here the Grand Master of the Teutonic Order von Knidprode paid his homage in the name of the monastic-knightly order. Catherine, in language similar to her mother's, warned the Grand Master not to neglect the monastic virtues of his order. She could foresee that by slow degeneration the Order might end in heresy. Indeed in 1525, the Grand Master Albrecht of Brandenburg led the Teutonic Order into Lutheranism. In Danzig, according to the legend, "a star appeared more radiant than the sun in its noontide splendor, and Birgitta's cortège followed the star to the seaport of Söderköping in East Gothland." In 1889, the German astronomer Wolff of Heidelberg named a star after Saint Birgitta. In front of the Cathedral of Linköping, Bishop Niels Hermansson, who once taught Latin grammar to Birgitta, sang his own hymn in honor of his spiritual friend. After twenty-five years Birgitta returned as the symbolic "mother and abbess of Vadstena," as Christ had promised her. For some two hundred years this Northern star was to shine over Sweden and Scandinavia. In Rome Countess Papazzuri wrote from her lonely palace, where Birgitta had lived and died, "I have been very melancholy lately, and in all my life I have never borne so great a sorrow in my heart."

More than anything Catherine preferred to stay at Vadstena close to the shrine of her mother Birgitta, but King Albrecht of Sweden and the bishops advised her to initiate the canonization. Returning to Rome, Catherine first healed a sinner, Venozza Orsini. When Florence revolted against the Papacy, Catherine pointed to Birgitta's prophecy in the *Revelations*, IV. 140. Then the Tiber River flooded the older sections of Rome, and Pope Gregory XI with the College of Cardinals visited *Domus Birgittae*, praying for an intercession. A miracle happened — the Tiber receded, and Gregory XI smiled, "Indeed, Catherine, you drank your mother's milk." But Catherine followed in the footsteps of the Blessed Mother of God and kept the "secrets of divine love" in her own heart. After the death of Pope Gregory XI, there was a tumult in front of Saint Peter's, the people demanding, "We must have a Roman or at least an Italian pope." Catherine remarked to Bishop Alphonse of Jaen, "Here is the Schism of which my mother Birgitta spoke." (Rev. III. 10)

Canonically elected to succeed Gregory XI was Pope Urban VI, a fierce Neapolitan who often quoted Birgitta's *Revelations* against the antipope Clement VII. Pope Urban VI initiated a Process of Canonization with an attest of fifty-one articles to the virtues, miracles and writings of Birgitta. Catherine, Sir Birger, Prior Peter Olafsson, Bishop Alphonse of Jaen, Archbishop Bernardi of Naples, Cardinal Eleazar de Sabran, Cardinal Niccolò Caracciolo, General Gomez Albornoz and Prince Latino Orsini all testified in behalf of Birgitta. As the Schism reached its height, interrupting the procedures, Catherine departed for Sweden. There she wrote a devotional book, *Consolation of the Soul,* and died shortly afterward. Another Neapolitan, Pope Boniface IX, canonized the Sibyl of the North in 1391 with the Bull *Ab Origine Mundi.* The indomitable Birgitta, who chided popes Clement VI, Innocent VI and Gregory XI for their weaknesses, had her name inscribed in the Golden Book of the Catholic saints. And, as it was prophesied in the beginning, "untold generations will praise her name."

Chapter III

NATIVITY OF OUR LORD

Nativity of Our Lord

To walk in the footsteps of Our Lord was a dream of every medieval Christian. As Birgitta arrived in Jerusalem, she remembered the words of Our Lady many years before: "Thou shalt come to the Holy City when so shall be the pleasure of my Son. From there thou shalt come to Bethlehem, where I will show unto thee in every particular how it happened when I gave birth to my Son in this place." (Rev. VII. 1) And now at the pool of Bethesda, where the house of Joachim and Anna once stood, Birgitta meditated on their marriage of love and the birth of the Virgin Mary, who revealed to her, "The truth is, that I was conceived without sin . . . that hour, therefore, in which I was conceived may well be called a golden hour, for then began the Salvation of mankind, and darkness gave way to light. This truth is, however, not known to many; one may even see pious people doubt it, until the time shall come when the truth shall be revealed." (Rev. VI. 49) Five hundred years later, on December 8, 1854, Pope Pius IX proclaimed this truth in dogma of the Immaculate Conception: "We declare, pronounce and define that the doctrine which holds that the most blessed Virgin Mary, in the first instant of her conception, by a singular grace and privilege granted by Almighty God in view of the merits of Jesus Christ, the Saviour of the human race, was preserved free from all stain of original sin, is a doctrine revealed by God and, therefore, to be believed firmly and constantly by all the faithful."

In Bethlehem at the grotto of Nativity, Birgitta prayed before the silver star inscribed with *Hic de Virgine Maria Jesus Christus natus est,* and meditated about the fullness of time when the Word became flesh. Knowing of the Gospel by Saint Luke, Birgitta, now lost in her mystical ecstacy, beheld a vision of the first Christmas Night in all its lyric tenderness: "When I was present by the manger of the Lord in Bethlehem, I beheld a Virgin of extreme beauty wrapped in a white mantle and a delicate tunic through which I perceived her virgin body soon to be delivered. With her was an old man of great honesty, and they brought with them an ox and a donkey. These entered the cave, and the man, after having tied them to the manger, went outside and brought to the Virgin a burning candle; having attached this to the wall, he went outside so that he might not be present at the birth. Then the Virgin pulled off her shoes from her feet, drew the white mantle that enveloped her, removed the veil from her head, laying it by her side, thus remaining in her tunic only with her beautiful golden hair falling loosely down her shoulders. Then she drew out two fine, clean linen cloths, and two of wool, which she had brought to wrap the newborn Child, and two smaller linen ones to cover and tie His head. These she laid beside her to use them in due time. When all these things were ready, then the Virgin, kneeling with great reverence, placed herself in prayer, with her back to the crib, her face eastward, raised to heaven. She stood with uplifted hands, her eyes fixed on heaven, rapt, as it were, in an ecstasy of contemplation, in a rapture of divine sweetness. And while she stood in prayer, I beheld her Child move in her womb and at once, in a twinkling of an eye, she brought forth her Son, from Whom such ineffable light and splendor radiated that the sun could not be compared to it; nor did the candle which the old man set in any manner give light, because that divine splendor had totally annihilated the material splendor of the candle, and so sudden and momentary was that mode of bearing that I could not perceive or discern how, or in what part she brought forth. Nevertheless, I immediately beheld that glorious babe lying naked and most pure on the ground, His flesh most clean from any kind of soil or impurity. Then I heard angelic chants of wonderful suavity and sweetness. When the Virgin felt that she already had born her Child, she immediately worshipped Him, her head bent down and her hands clasped, with great reverence, and said unto Him, 'Be welcome my God, my Lord and my Son!' Then the Child, crying and, as it were, shivering with cold from the hard floor where He lay, turned a little and stretched out His limbs, seeking to find His mother's warmth and love. The mother then took Him in her arms and pressed Him to her breast, and with her cheek and her breast she warmed Him with great joy and tender maternal compassion. She then sat down on the floor and laid the Child in her lap, and at once she began to bestow upon Him much care, tying up His small body, His legs and His arms with long cloths, first the linen garments and then the woolen ones. Then she enveloped the head of the Child, tying it up with two linen garments. When this was done, the old man entered and, prostrating himself on the floor, wept for joy. And in no way was the Virgin changed by the birth, neither as to the color of her face nor as to any illness, and her bodily strength did not decline, as is usually the case with women when they bear. Then she stood up, carrying the Child in her arms, and together the two, she and Joseph, put Him into the manger, and on their knees they worshipped Him with immense joy and happiness. And then I heard the wonderful singing of many angels." (Rev. VII. 21)

And then Mary, as a Mother to a mother, reassured Birgitta that this was the way Jesus was born: "My daughter, know that I bore my Son as you have seen, praying alone on my knees in the stable. I bore Him with such a joy and exultation of mind that I felt no pain or difficulty when He left my body. But I immediately wrapped Him in clean swaddling clothes which I had previously prepared. When Joseph saw this, he wondered with great joy that I had been delivered without any aid. As the great multitude of people in Bethlehem were busy with the census, the wonders of God could not be divulged among them. And, therefore, know truly that although men, according to human ideas, would assert my Son was born in a usual way, it is true beyond all doubt that He was born as I tell you and as you have seen.'' (Rev. VII. 23)

The Virgin Mary, knowing the prophecies to be fulfilled and understanding the angel when he appeared to her in the Annunciation revealing that the fullness of time was nearing, shared with Birgitta her intimate feelings about the Incarnation: "I did not need purification, like other women, because my Son Who was born of me made me clean. Nor did I contract the least stain. Nevertheless, that the Law and the prophecies might be fulfilled, I chose to live according to the Law. Nor did I live like worldly parents, nor did I wish to show anything extraordinary in me, but loved whatever was humble. On that day my pain, as today, was increased. For though, by divine inspiration, I knew that my Son was to suffer, this grief pierced my heart more keenly at Simeon's words, when he said that the sword would pierce my soul, and that my Son should be prepared for a sign to be contradicted. And until I was assumed in body and soul to heaven, this grief never left my heart, although it was tempered by the consolation of the spirit of God.'' (Rev. VI. 57)

Birgitta, as a follower of Saint Bernard, knew of his devotion to the Nativity of Our Lord. She was aware of Saint Francis' introducing the crèche into the Christmas celebration, and she must have read Pseudo-Bonaventura's *Meditations* as the most explanatory writings about the Nativity. For almost half a century Birgitta meditated over the birth of Christ, and on her pilgrimages she keenly observed the portrayals of the Nativity. Now at the very manger where the Incarnation took place Birgitta beheld her own vision, which surpassed all previous interpretations. It was Birgitta's *Revelations* which influenced Western art, music and literature and even the decisions at the Council of Trent, serving as a guideline for the arts.

When Birgitta described the Virgin Mary kneeling with her golden hair falling over her shoulders, Joseph entering the manger with a candle, the ineffable light radiating from the Christ Child, the words of greeting, "Be welcome my God, my Lord and my Son" and the singing of the angels, she introduced a new element which led to a new style of portraying the Nativity. In the previous Italo-Byzantine style Our Lady was portrayed sitting, reclining or lying on the bed, and Joseph was dozing in the corner, symbolizing humanity not aware of the Incarnation. Yet the animals, the ox and the donkey, knelt reverently and blew out of their nostrils to warm the Christ Child. There was no light radiating from His body.

The Pseudo-Bonaventura interpretation of the Nativity showed Our Lady leaning against a broken column and delivering the Child. Both styles and interpretations were not acceptable to the spiritually minded Birgitta. In the high Middle Ages the Virgin Mary was idealized, so the prevalent Mariology favored Birgitta's interpretation.

Birgitta brought her *Revelations* to Naples. Prince Orsini testified in the Process of Canonization that immediately after Birgitta's departure from Naples in 1373 he already saw in the Church of Saint Anthony a large painting of Nativity according to the vision of Saint Birgitta. The new style only proved that the written word influences the other arts and does not necessarily restrain them. Unfortunately for history this oldest painting of its kind got lost, but in the Basilica Santa Maria Novella in Florence there is an important fresco by the Lorenzetti School portraying the Nativity scene. Instead of signing it, the artist paid tribute to Birgitta as the source by portraying her as a pilgrim in the right-hand corner. Yet this Nativity represents a cross-road between the Byzantine, Pseudo-Bonaventura interpretation and the Birgittine style because the ox and the donkey are kneeling, although all the rest is portrayed strictly according to Birgitta. The painting heralded the new style in Nativity presentation. The wood panel by Niccolò di Tommaso in the Pinacoteca Vaticana faithfully follows the *Revelations* and is now the oldest of its kind. Tommaso was followed by Turino Vanni of Siena, whose wood panel is now in San Matteo Museum in Pisa and is the second oldest of its kind. Nativity by Sano di Pietro in Pinacoteca Vaticana and another by an unknown South German artist in Constance opened the door for the international style of idealization and spiritualization of Fra Angelico, Lippi, Botticelli, Memling, Francke, Dürer, Grünewald, Correggio and Rembrandt. Through the centuries the strictly Birgittine fifteenth-century style evolved through new techniques of color, light and perspective. But the essence of Birgitta's style was preserved as the seventeenth-century Neapolitan crèche proves. Known for its beauty and bucolic dramatization the crèche is an elaborated Nativity according to Birgitta. The seventeenth-century Saint Alphonse di Liguori of Naples brought Birgitta's *Revelations* to the renewed attention of Italy. And so three hundred years after Birgitta's sojourn in Naples, the seeds of her revelation of Nativity were still bearing fruit in a well-developed industry of crèches.

The Iconography of Nativity became a real issue at the Council of Trent in 1564. Throughout the centuries art was sponsored by the Church, and from time to time style was questioned from the theological, devotional and esthetic points of view. Challenged by Protestantism and the new spirit of the time, Jesuit Johannes Molanus purged the Iconography. The Byzantine style depicting Our Lady tired and sick after the birth or sitting or reclining on the bed was considered in poor taste. Birgitta's style of a happy, healthy Virgin Mary kneeling in adoration of the Christ Child was accepted. Women portrayed helping Mary with the birth or washing the Child, which were accepted according to the older theology, were now rejected by the Council of Trent as the Virgin Mary, according to the *Revelations*, gave birth to the Christ Child without any help. The bath was unnecessary because the Virgin's conception was immaculate, Christ Himself having been sent by the Father to purify humanity of the stain of sin with His blood. From the esthetic point of view duplication of a crib and a bath was confusing and difficult to portray as the Nativity by Giotto's pupil in Assisi proved. A new trend in art required the composition to center around the adoration of the Christ Child. Pseudo-Bonaventura's idea of the Virgin Mary's bearing the Child by leaning against the column — actually the idea is taken from Greek mythology and ancient practices — and Joseph's at the last moment putting some hay at the feet of Mary was considered repugnant regardless of how realistic it might sound. Instead, Our Lady's taking her shoes off — as Moses did when speaking to God through the burning bush — was accepted as a sign of reverence. In the Byzantine style there was no candle to show the way through spiritual darkness; Birgitta introduced the candle which was only to be overpowered by the Divine Light radiating from Christ's body. In their Nativity scenes, Correggio and Rembrandt and Tintoretto accentuated divinity over humanity through the use of light. According to Birgitta, the Christ Child is almost floating above the earth. The Nativity scenes were usually placed at the altar, and the Christ Child would appear to be coming out of the chalice during the Communion.

The idea of a cave was retained in Western art. Originally the cave symbolized the birth and burial place of Christ. The Three Kings who had prostrated themselves in the Byzantine style, in Western art genuflected, paying feudal homage. They symbolized the kings of this earth acknowledging the sovereignty of the Heavenly King. When the Americas were discovered, a Portuguese artist attempted to introduce a fourth king in the person of an Indian chieftain of Brazil, but the Church reserved its approval. The ox and the donkey were supposed to be removed from the Iconography of Nativity, but Isaiah's and Birgitta's writings were well-imbedded in the popular and artistic mind.

The Gospels are too scant in describing the Nativity. Birgitta's *Revelations* preserved the Gospels' orthodoxy, yet expanded them as a source of artistic inspiration. Birgitta brought a noble, poetic and spiritualized style to Nativity. The previous gross, trivial and even common approach, because it did not edify the souls of the faithful, was abandoned. Birgitta's influence on art pertaining to the Nativity and Crucifixion is of transcendental importance. Some zealots at the Council of Basel suggested her *Revelations* be incorporated into the Bible itself.

IN HONOR OF THE BLESSED VIRGIN MARY
prayer by Saint Birgitta

Blessed and venerated be thou, my Lady Virgin Mary, most holy Mother of God, Whose noblest creature thou art, and Who was never so loved as by thee, O glorious Lady.

Glory be to thee, my Lady Virgin Mary, who was announced to thy father and mother by the same angel who announced Christ to thee.

Blessed be thou, my Lady Virgin Mary, who in thy most holy infancy, immediately after leaving thy mother's breasts, was borne by thy parents to God's temple.

Praise be to thee, my Lady Virgin Mary, who was totally inflamed with the ardor of divine love, when the angel of God came to thee, and announced to thee the will of God. And thou replying, didst most humbly declare thyself the handmaiden of God; and the Holy Ghost wonderfully filled thee with all virtue. And so, in that blessed hour, the Son of God became in thee thy Son, living with all His members, yet not losing His divine Majesty.

Blessed be thou, my Lady Virgin Mary, who dist constantly feel the body of Christ, created of thy blessed body, grow and move in thy womb till the time of His glorious Nativity; Whom thou before all others didst touch with thy sacred hands, wrap up in clothes, and, according to the prophecy, didst lay in a manger and didst maternally nurture.

Glory be to thee, O my Lady Virgin Mary, who, inhabiting a humble stable, didst see powerful kings come from afar, with great humility and reverence offering royal gifts to thy Son; Whom afterwards thou didst present with precious hands in the temple, and during

35

Whose infancy thou didst diligently preserve in thy blessed heart all things seen and heard.

Blessed be thou, my Lady Virgin Mary, who didst fly to Egypt with thy most holy Son, Whom thou didst afterwards bring with joy to Nazareth, and behold Him, thy Son, as He grew bodily, humble and obedient to thee and Joseph.

Blessed be thou, my Lady Virgin Mary, who didst behold thy Son preaching, working miracles, and choosing His Apostles, who, enlightened by His example, miracles and teaching, were made witnesses of the truth, announcing to all nations that thy Jesus was truly the Son of God, that it was He Who had accomplished in Himself the oracles of the prophets, when He patiently endured a most atrocious death for the human race.

Blessed be thou, my Lady Virgin Mary, who didst beforehand know that thy Son was to be arrested, and didst afterward, with thy blessed eyes, mournfully see Him bound and scourged, crowned with thorns and fastened naked to the Cross.

Honor be to thee, my Lady Virgin Mary, who didst woefully hear with thy blessed ears thy Son speaking to thee in pain from the Cross and crying to His Father in the agony of death, and commending His soul to His Father's hands.

Praise be to thee, my Lady Virgin Mary, who in bitter grief didst behold thy Son hanging on the Cross, livid and stained with His own blood, His glorious side transpierced and all His skin torn without mercy.

Blessed be thou, my Lady Virgin Mary, who with tearful eyes didst behold thy Son taken down, wrapped in winding sheets, laid in the sepulchre, and there guarded by soldiers.

Rejoice, my most worthy Lady Virgin Mary, that the very moment thy Son rose from the dead, He wished it to be known to thee, His most Blessed Mother, because He at once appeared in person to thee, then showed to others that He, Who underwent death in His living body, was risen from the dead.

Rejoice, then, my most worthy Lady Virgin Mary, who, having seen death conquered, and the way to heaven laid open, didst see thy Son rising triumphant with the crown of victory; and on the fortieth day after His Resurrection, didst behold Him honorably ascend to His heavenly kingdom.

Exult, my most worthy Lady Virgin Mary, that thou didst deserve to see how thy Son, after His Ascension, sent down on His Apostles and disciples the Holy Ghost, and, with Whom He increased in His followers the fervor of charity and faith.

Rejoice, my Lady Virgin Mary, and let the whole earth rejoice with thy joy, that thy Son permitted thee to remain many years in this world after His Ascension, to console His friends and strengthen them in faith, to help the needy, and sagely to counsel the Apostles.

Blessed be thou, my Lady Virgin Mary, who from thy ardent charity and maternal love didst unceasingly desire to join thy beloved Son, now sitting in heaven; and thou, living in this world but sighing for heavenly things, didst humbly conform thyself to the divine will, whereby, as divine justice dictates, thou didst indescribably increase thy eternal glory.

Eternal honor and glory be to thee, my Lady Virgin Mary, who, when the angel of God announced His intention to take thee from the exile of this world and to honor thy soul eternally in His kingdom, wished thy venerable body to be interned by the Apostles.

Rejoice, O my Lady Virgin Mary, that in thy calm death thy soul was embraced by the power of God, Who, paternally guarding thy soul, protected it from all adversity. And then God the Father subjected all creation to thy power; and the Son of God honorably placed thee, His most worthy Mother, on a high throne beside Him; and the Holy Ghost wonderfully exalted thee to His glorious kingdom, a Virgin espoused to Himself.

Exult, O Mother of God, glorious Lady Virgin Mary, that thou didst deserve to see thy body quickened after death, assumed with thy soul with angelic honors to heaven, and that thou didst see with exultation thy glorious Son, God with humanity, to be the most just judge of all men, and rewarder of good works.

Rejoice also, my Lady Virgin Mary, that the sacred flesh of thy body knew that it existed as Virgin Mother in heaven, and knew itself to be immaculate from all mortal and venial stain; nay, knew that thou hadst done all virtuous deeds out of so much love that it behooved God to exalt thee with the highest honor. Then also didst thou understand that who so loves God most ardently in this world will be placed nearest to Him in heaven.

Blessed be thou, O my Lady Virgin Mary, that every faithful creature praises the Trinity for thee, because thou art His most worthy creature, who doest most promptly obtain pardon for wretched souls, who art the most faithful advocate for all sinners.

Praised then be God, supreme Lord, Who created thee to such great honor, that thou shouldst become Queen in the Kingdom of Heaven, to reign with Him eternally through ages and ages, Amen.

Chapter IV

CRUCIFIXION OF OUR LORD

Crucifixion of Our Lord

Throughout her life Birgitta followed in the footsteps of Our Lord. Now at seventy she climbed her last thorny path to Golgotha to relive the Passion of Christ. She could hear the hammer strokes over the nails on the Cross and see the plunge of the lance into the heart of Our Saviour. Birgitta's whole being was consumed in a prayer: "My Lord Jesus, You are a Divine Knight Who led the people out of the darkness of suffering into eternal joy, because with the blood of Your heart, You opened Paradise for mankind." A diminishing whisper from the Cross, "It is finished," made Birgitta realize that her life in the service of the Lord was finished too. As Christ was obedient to the Father until death, Birgitta as a bride was obedient to Christ. Here at Golgotha itself, she found her Holy Grail with the precious blood shed for the Salvation of mankind. Birgitta, therefore, was blessed with another vision of Christ, which as authentic poetry with a biblical flavor is still a favorite Good Friday reading and meditation.

"While I was at Mount Calvary weeping bitterly, I beheld my Lord, naked and scourged, led out by the soldiers to be crucified, and diligently guarded by them. I then beheld, too, a hole cut in the mountain, and the crucifiers around, ready to perform their cruel work. But my Lord, turning to me, said, 'Observe, that in this hollow of the rock was the foot of My Cross planted, at the time of My Passion,' and I immediately saw how the Cross was fixed there by the enemies, and fastened firmly in the hollow of the rock of the mountain, with wooden pegs driven in on all sides by mallets, so that the Cross should stand solidly, and not fall. Now when the Cross was firmly planted there, boards were set around the main piece of the Cross like steps, as high as where the feet of a crucified person would be, so that he and the crucifiers might ascend by these steps, and stand more conveniently on them during the crucifixion.

"Then they ascended those steps, leading my Lord with the greatest scoffing and insult. Joyfully ascending, like a gentle lamb led to the slaughter, once He was on those steps, He extended His arm, not forced, but voluntarily, and opening His right hand, He laid it upon the Cross, and His cruel torturers barbarously crucified it, driving the nail through the part where the bone was most solid. Then violently drawing His left hand with a rope, they affixed it to the Cross in a similar manner. Then stretching His body beyond all bounds, they fastened His joined feet to the Cross with two nails, and violently extended those glorious limbs on the Cross so that almost all His nerves and veins were broken. This done, they replaced on His head the crown of thorns, which they had taken off while affixing Him to the Cross, and fastened it on His most sacred head. It so wounded His venerable head that His eyes were filled with the blood that flowed down. His ears, too, were closed, and His face and beard covered and stained with that rosy blood. His crucifiers removed all the boards placed up against the Cross, and then the Cross remained alone and lofty with my Lord crucified upon it.

And when I beheld their cruelty, full of grief, then I beheld His most dolorous Mother, as it were, trembling and half-dead with John and her sisters, who stood not far from the Cross on the right, consoling her. My new pain of compassion for that most holy Mother so transfixed me that I felt as if a sharp sword of insupportable bitterness pierced my heart. At length his dolorous Mother rose, lifeless in body, and looked on her Son, and stood thus supported by her sisters, overwhelmed with stupor, as if pierced with a sword of grief.

"When her Son beheld her and His friends weeping, He commended her in a mournful voice to John, and one could discern by His gesture and voice that His heart was pierced by the most keen dart of immense sorrow. Then His loving and beautiful eyes took the hue of death; His mouth opened and appeared full of blood; His countenance was pallid and sunken, livid and blood-stained; His body was also livid and pallid, and very weak from the constant stream of flowing blood. His skin also, the virginal flesh of that most holy body, was so delicate and tender that a livid welt appeared from the slightest blow. Sometimes He endeavored to stretch Himself upon the Cross, from the intense and acute pain that He endured, for sometimes the pain from His members and pierced veins ascended to His heart and tortured Him cruelly with the prolonged death. Overcome by the excessive bitterness of His suffering, and about to expire, He cried out to His Father in a loud and mournful voice, 'My God, My God, why hast Thou forsaken Me?' Then, His lips pallid, and His tongue blood-stained, His stomach collapsed and clinging to His back, as though He had no entrails within Him, again He cried out in great grief and anguish, "Father, into Thy hands I commend My spirit." Then His head raised a little, then sank, and He gave up the ghost.

"His Mother, seeing this, trembled all over, and would have fallen to the ground in her bitter anguish, had she not been supported by the other women. At that hour, His hands shrunk a little from the place of the piercing, in consequence of the great weight of His body, which now rested almost entirely on the nails with which the feet were attached to the Cross. But His fingers and hands and arms were more extended than before; His shoulders and back were pressed on the Cross.

"Finally, some of the people around mockingly cried against His Mother, saying many things. Some said, "Mary, thy Son is dead." Others spoke more jeering words, and then, while the crowd stood around, one running up with great fury plunged a lance into His right side so powerfully that the lance seemed about to come forth from the opposite side of His body, and when it was drawn out, a very river of blood gushed impetuously from that wound. The lance head and part of the handle came forth blood-stained. His Mother, seeing this, trembled so violently and with such bitter groans, her countenance and manner showed that her soul was then pierced with a keen sword of grief.

"After this, when the crowd had departed, His friends took down Our Lord, Whom His pious Mother received in her holy arms, and she held Him on her knee, all wounded, torn and livid; and then His dolorous Mother wiped His whole body and His wounds with her veil, and closed His eyes, kissing them, and wrapped Him in a clean winding-sheet, and thus they bore Him, with great wailing and grief, and laid Him in the sepulchre." (Rev. VII. 15)

Birgitta's narration of the Crucifixion is a drama spoken in a biblical language. One is transported to the scene of Golgotha overlooking Jerusalem to witness the supreme event in history. It is the Sorrowful Mother now, who with a loving tenderness reveals to Birgitta the suffering of her Son on the Cross. The nuances in the two descriptions of the Crucifixion inspired artists, composers and the men of letters through the centuries. Indeed, divine inspiration guided Birgitta's pen.

The Mother of God revealed to Birgitta the Crucifixion of her Son: "As often as I looked at my Son, as often as I wrapped Him in His swaddling clothes, as often as I saw His hands and feet, so often was my soul absorbed in fresh grief, for I thought of how He would be crucified. When suckling Him, I thought of the gall and vinegar; when swathing Him, of the cords with which He was to be bound; when bearing Him in my arms, of the Cross to which He was to be nailed; when sleeping, of His death."

"And as He stood there bound to the pillar, He had no garments on at all, but was as naked as when He had come into the world, and He suffered shame that He had to endure this. Then all my Son's friends fled from Him, and His enemies surrounded Him and tore His body that was so pure and without blemish and without any infection or sin. But I, who was standing near, fell down like one dead at the sound of the first blow. And when I came to myself, I saw His body beaten and torn, so that the ribs could be seen. And what was still more dreadful to see was that when scourges were withdrawn, His flesh was torn like the earth by a plough. . . . And when I came to the place of torment I saw everything made ready for His death . . . But when I heard the blow of the last nail being struck, it grew dark before my eyes; my hands and feet shook, and I fell to the ground. When I rose again, I saw my Son hanging there so miserably. So did my Son stand on the Cross, wounded and bleeding; only His heart was sound, for it was of the best and strongest nature, for from my flesh He had taken the very purest body. And because His nature was of the very best, life and death struggled a long while in His wounded body . . . For sometimes the pains from His torn body went up to the heart, which was the strongest part of Him, and sometimes the pains again darted into limbs, and the agony of death was long and bitter."

"And as my Son was suffering thus, He looked down at His weeping friends, who would rather have endured all His agony or burn forever in hell, than see Him thus in suffering. And His sorrow over the sorrow of His friends was more than all the other pain in either His limbs or His heart, for He loved His friends exceedingly. But now when His fear and torment was becoming greater than He could endure, He cried to His Father and said, 'Father, into Thy hands I commend My spirit.' And when I, His Mother, heard this cry, all my limbs trembled in my heart's bitterest need, and afterwards, every time I thought of it, it was as if I heard those words again. But now, when death came and His heart broke, all His limbs trembled, and His head rose up a little and then bowed down again. His mouth was open, His tongue full of blood; His fingers and arms shrank a little. His back fell hard on the Cross. Then someone said to me, 'Mary, your Son is dead, but He shall surely rise from the dead.' Then they all went away, but one came and thrust a spear into His side. And when the spear was drawn out, the point was red with blood, and it was to me as if my own heart was cut asunder. Thereafter He was taken down from the Cross, and I laid Him over my knees, and He looked like a leper. His eyes were glazed and full of blood, His mouth cold as snow, His beard like grass, His face shrunken; His arms had grown so stiff that they could not bend farther down than to the navel. As He hung on the Cross, so I had Him upon my knees, and He was like a man who is crippled in all His limbs. Then they laid Him in a clean linen shroud, and I closed His eyes and His mouth, for they were open. After that they laid Him in the sepulchre. Oh, my daughter, how willingly would I have gone into the grave with Him, if this had been His will. When this was done, the good John came and took me home. Behind us we left the Cross standing high and alone." (Rev. VI. 57-58)

Matthias Grünewald as an artist, mystic and theologian concurred with Dante's dictum that art is the language which translates dogma into form. The Isenheim Altar consists of the Nativity and Crucifixion according to Saint Birgitta, and the Resurrection. The theme of the Crucifixion is, "The Lamb of God which taketh away the sin of the world," and Saint John the Baptist is mystically introduced into the scene pointing to Christ Crucified, Who is out of proportion with the painting itself: "He must increase but I must decrease." (Jn, 3:30) The rest is portrayed literally according to Birgitta's vision: "And then the crown of thorns was pressed tightly on His head, descending to the middle of His forehead, many streams of blood flowing down His face . . . the fingers painfully pointing upwards, for the nails were driven where the bone in the hand was hardest and firmest . . . His feet were curled around the nails as around door hinges." (Rev. IV. 70)

The body of Christ is full of splinters symbolizing the sins of mankind. Even the Cross is bending under the weight of sins that the Saviour has taken upon Himself to redeem mankind. According to Saint Birgitta, there were over five thousand wounds, splinters and cuts in the holy body of Christ. Grünewald's Crucifixion is therefore not just another illustration or record of an event, but a symbolism of theology. Tintoretto brought a cosmic awareness and Rembrandt an exceeding humaneness into their Crucifixions, but they could not penetrate into the meaning behind the appearance as did Grünewald with his unique work, the final religious and mystical outburst in art.

Equally unique, timeless and beyond any comparison is Pietà of the Avignon School in 1460. Pietà, in which the Sorrowful Mother adores the dead body of Christ Crucified, is described by Birgitta: "The friends of the Lord took Him down from the Cross, and His dolorous Mother took Him in her holy arms and laid Him upon her knees . . . she dried His whole body and all His wounds with a linen cloth . . . and laid Him in the sepulchre." (Rev. VII. 15) Then the Mother of God revealed to Birgitta: "His hands were so stiffened that they could not be raised above the navel. As He stood on the Cross, so I held Him in my arms, like a man contracting in every limb." (Rev. I. 10) From the Avignon Pietà to Michelangelo's Pietà, all followed Birgitta's interpretation.

Birgitta's vision of Golgotha can be reviewed in the masterpieces by van Eyck, Weyden, Memling, Pacher, Multscher, Wohlgemuth, Schäufelin, Dürer, Vischer, Mantegna, Botticelli, Titian, Tintoretto, El Greco and Rembrandt. Yet Pietà of the Avignon School and the Crucifixion by Grünewald in 1517 exceed everything beyond any comparison. Vischer the "Birgittenmeister" in sculpture, Bach with the *Passion According to Saint John*, Clemens Brentano in prose with the *Sufferings of Christ*, and Abraham de Santa Clara in rhetoric all followed Birgitta's *Revelations*. Birgitta was often called the Fulfiller of the New Testament.

IN HONOR OF OUR LORD JESUS CHRIST
prayer by Saint Birgitta

O Jesus Christ, eternal sweetness of those who find hope in Thee, joy exceeding all joy and all desire, Saviour and lover of sinners, Who hast declared it Thy delight to be among the children of men, made man for man in the end of time; remember all Thy inner grief, which

Thou didst endure in Thy human body at the approach of the time of Thy most saving Passion, preordained in Thy divine heart. Remember the sadness and the bitterness, which, as Thou Thyself didst testify, Thou didst feel in Thy soul, when at the Last Supper with Thy disciples Thou didst give them Thy Body and Blood, wash their feet, and, sweetly consoling them, didst foretell Thy imminent Passion. Remember all the fear, anguish, and grief which Thou didst endure in Thy body before the Passion on the Cross; when after Thy thrice-repeated prayer and bloody sweat, Thou was betrayed by Thy disciple Judas, accused by false witnesses, unjustly judged by three judges, condemned although innocent in the chosen city at paschal time, in the bloom of youth, stripped of Thy own robes and clothed in the garments of another, buffeted, Thy face and eyes veiled, smitten with blows, bound to the pillar, scourged, crowned with thorns, struck with a reed on the head, and torn with numberless acts of violence. Give me, O Lord God, I beseech Thee, before I die, in memory of these Thy Passions on the Cross, a true contrition, true confession, worthy satisfaction, and remission of all my sins.

O Jesus, maker of the world, Whom no measure doth encompass, Who enclosest the earth in Thy palm, remember the most bitter grief which Thou didst endure when the soldiers fastened Thy most sacred hands to the Cross with dull nails, and, as Thou was agreeable to their will, added pain to pain by perforating Thy most delicate feet, and cruelly wrenching and distending Thee the length and breadth of Thy Cross, so that the joints of Thy limbs were loosened. I beseech Thee by the memory of this most sacred and bitter pain on the Cross to fill me with Thy fear and love.

O Jesus, heavenly physician, remember the languor, lividness and pain which Thou didst suffer on the lofty scaffold on the Cross, torn in all Thy limbs, not one of which remained in its right state, so that Thy pain was like no other, for from the sole of Thy foot to the top of Thy head there was no soundness in Thee. And yet, regardless of all pains, Thou didst piously pray to Thy Father for Thy enemies, say-ing, *"Father, forgive them, for they know not what they do."* By this mercy and in remembrance of that pain, grant that my memory of Thy most bitter Passion be a full remission of all my sins.

O Jesus, true liberty of angels, paradise of delights, remember the grief and horror which Thou didst endure, when all Thy enemies surrounded Thee like fierce lions and tortured Thee by buffets, spit-ting upon Thee, tearing Thy flesh. By these pains and all the con-tumelious words and most severe torments, O Lord Jesus Christ, whereby all Thy enemies afflicted Thee, I beg Thee to release me from all enemies, visible and invisible, and to grant me the perfection of eternal Salvation under the shadow of Thy wings.

O Jesus, mirror of eternal light, remember Thy grief of those to be saved by the merits of Thy Passion, and the reprobation of the wicked, to be damned by their own demerits; and by the abyss of Thy mercy, with which Thou didst then embrace all lost and hopeless sinners, mercy which Thou didst show the thief on the cross, saying, *"This day thou shalt be with Me in paradise."* I beseech Thee, O merci-ful Jesus, show mercy to me at the hour of my death.

O Jesus, amiable king and most desirable friend, remember the sorrow Thou hadst, when Thou didst hang naked and wretched on the Cross, and all Thy friends and enemies stood under Thee, and Thou didst find no comforter except Thy beloved Mother, most faithfully standing by Thee in the bitterness of her soul, whom Thou didst com-mend to Thy disciple John, saying, *"Woman, behold Thy son!"* I beseech Thee, merciful Jesus, by the sword of grief which then pierced Thy soul, have compassion on me in all my tribulations and afflictions, bodily and spiritual, and give me comfort at the hour of my death.

O Jesus, fountain of inexhaustible mercy, Who from intense feel-ing didst exclaim on the Cross, *"I thirst!"* — thirsting for the Salvation of the human race; inflame, we beseech Thee, the desire of our hearts to every perfect work, and extinguish in us the heat of carnal longings and worldly delights.

O Jesus, sweetness of hearts and great sweetness of minds, by the bitterness of the vinegar and gall which Thou didst taste for us, grant me at the hour of my death worthily to receive Thy Body and Blood, for the remedy and consolation of my soul.

O Jesus, royal virtue and mental delight, remember the anguish and pain which Thou didst endure when, from the bitterness of death and the reproaches of Thy enemies, Thou didst exclaim in loud voice that Thou was forsaken by Thy Father, saying, *"My God, My God, why hast Thou forsaken Me?"* By this anguish, I beseech Thee not to forsake me in my anguish, O Lord our God.

O Jesus, most profound abyss of mercy, I beseech Thee by the depth of Thy wounds, which pierced Thy vitals and the marrow of Thy bones, raise me from the depth of sin in which I am plunged, and hide me in the hollow of Thy wounds, from the face of Thy wrath, till Thy anger pass away.

O Jesus, mirror of truth, sign of unity, and bond of charity, remember Thy innumerable wounds wherewith Thou was reddened with Thy most sacred blood, and the magnitude of pain Thou didst endure on Thy virginal flesh for us. O merciful Jesus, what more shouldst Thou do, and hast not done? Engrave, I beseech Thee, O merciful Jesus, all Thy wounds in my heart with Thy most precious blood, that in them I may read Thy sorrow and death, and in thanksgiving persevere duly to the end.

O Jesus, most valiant lion, immortal and unconquered king, remember the pain which Thou didst endure, when all powers of Thy heart and body failed Thee, and, inclining Thy head, Thou didst exclaim, *"It is consumated!"* By that anguish and pain, remember me in the last consumation of my departure, when my soul shall be in anguish and my spirit troubled.

O Jesus, only begotten Son of the most high Father, splendor and figure of His substance, remember Thou didst commend Thy spirit to Thy Father, saying, *"Into Thy hands, O Lord, I commend My spirit!"* And then, with lacerated body and broken heart, with a loud cry, the breasts of Thy mercy exposed, Thou didst expire to redeem us. By this precious death, I beseech Thee, O king of saints, comfort me to resist the devil, the world and the flesh and blood, that, dead to the world, I may live in Thee; and in the last hour of my departure, receive Thou my exiled, wandering spirit as it returns to Thee.

O Jesus, true and fruitful vine, remember the overflowing and abundant effusion of blood, which poured in torrents, like wine pressed from the grape, when on the press of the Cross Thou didst tread alone, and Thy side having been opened with a lance, Thou didst pour forth to us blood and water, so that not the least drop remained in Thee; and at last Thou was suspended on high like a bundle of myrrh, Thy delicate flesh faded, the moisture of Thy members and the marrow of Thy bones dried up. By this most bitter Passion and the effusion of Thy precious blood, I pray Thee, receive my soul in the agony of my death.

O sweet Jesus, wound my heart, that tears of penitence and love may be my food night and day, and bring me entirely to Thee, that my heart may ever be habitable for Thee, and my conversation pleasing and acceptable to Thee, and the end of my life so praiseworthy, that after the close of this life, I may deserve to praise Thee forever.

O Lord Jesus Christ, Son of the living God, receive this prayer in that most exceeding love, wherewith Thou didst bear all the wounds of Thy most sacred body; and remember me Thy servant; and to all sinners, and the faithful, living and dead, give mercy, grace, remission and eternal life, Amen.

José Drudis Biada, 1966   *Los Angeles, California*

SAINT BIRGITTA OF SWEDEN

*"This is the woman who is to come from
the country farthest to the North and who shall teach
wisdom to countless nations."*

PROCESSUS, P. 480

R. Werner, xx c.   *Vadstena, Sweden*

THE FIRST VISION OF MARY

*Our Lady appeared to seven years old Birgitta offering
her a crown with seven precious stones. The seven virtues
guided Birgitta throughout her life on her path to Salvation.*

Swedish Art, xv c.   *Stockholm Museum*

THE FIRST VISION OF CHRIST

"Oh my dearest Lord, who has ill-treated You so?"
"All they who forgot Me and despise My love."

Giuseppe Montanari, XVIII C.   *In Panisperna, Rome*

BRIDE OF CHRIST

"I am speaking not only to you but to all Christians.
You will be My bride . . . and it shall be
through you that I will speak to the world. My spirit will
dwell in you until your death."

✥

EXTRAV. 47

Biagio Puccini, XVIII C.   *Domus Birgittae, Rome*

CHRIST IS MY LOVE

*"I am happy to obey what is commanded to me for love of Him
Who obeyed His Father unto death."*

✦

REV. VI. 49

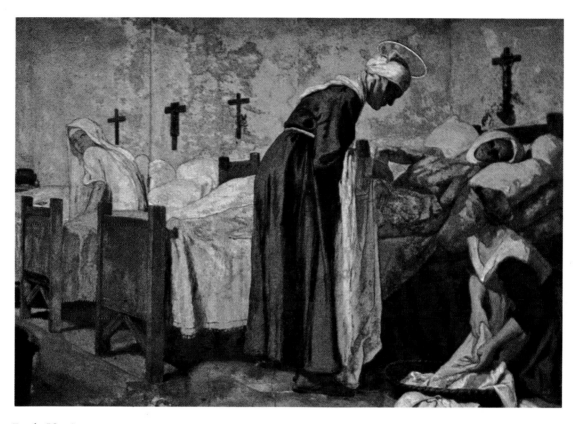

Paolo Vetri, xx c.   *St. Birgitta Church, Naples*

A LADY OF CHARITY

Princess Birgitta established a private hospital,
a hospice for the aged and an orphanage for abandoned children,
always taking personal interest in the poor
as a true Samaritan.

✦

CHIMINELLI, LA MISTICA DEL NORD

Fra Bartolomeo, XVI C.   *Academy, Florence*

BIRGITTA BESTOWS THE RULES

*In order to regenerate the spiritual and moral life
of Sweden and Europe, Birgitta founded in 1346 the Religious Order
of the Holy Saviour in Vadstena, a double
monastery for nuns and monks.*

Brussels School, xv c.   *Frankfurt, Germany*

ANGEL OF ROME

"Saint Birgitta is the most illustrious pilgrim
who lived within the walls of Rome . . .
this woman of royal blood, the energetic counsellor of
four popes, was certainly one of the greatest
religious women who ever lived."

—✦—

THESEIDER, HISTORY OF ROME

German Renaissance, xv c.   *National Museum, Nuremberg*

AMBASSADRESS OF GOD

"Birgitta was of an indomitable, aristocratic spirit,
always remaining a noblewoman to whom it came
naturally to speak and write the truth to
the princes of State and Church."

✧

NILSSON, HISTORY OF SWEDEN

Lorenzetti School, XIV C.   *S. Maria Novella, Florence*

HAIL, MARY, FULL OF GRACE

*The Nativity scene with Birgitta as a pilgrim
represents the crossroad between the Pseudo-Bonaventura* Meditations
and Saint Birgitta's Revelations *as a
source of interpretation. The fresco was damaged
during the flood in 1966.*

Niccolò di Tommaso, XIV c.   *Pinacoteca Vaticana, Rome*

"BE WELCOME MY GOD, MY LORD AND MY SON"

*The above greeting . . . Mary's kneeling in prayer . . .
her hair down her shoulders . . . the ineffable light from the Christ Child . . .
Joseph in reverence . . . angels singing . . . all this
is original with Birgitta.*

Leonardo da Vinci, xv c.   *Uffizi, Florence*

MADONNA ACCORDING TO SAINT BIRGITTA

*"I beheld a Virgin of extreme beauty wrapped in a white
mantle . . . her beautiful golden hair falling loosely down her shoulders . . .
the Virgin removed her shoes from her feet . . . and took the Child
in her arms with love and tender compassion."*

—◆—

REV.VII.21

Titian, XVI C.   *Prado, Madrid*

SAINT BIRGITTA'S MADONNA

"After Rome and Jerusalem . . . thou shalt come to Bethlehem,
where I will show unto thee in every particular how it happened,
when I gave birth to my Son in this place."

✧

REV. VII.1

Matthias Grünewald, XVI c.　　　　　　　　　　　　　　*Museum in Colmar, France*

CRUCIFIXION ACCORDING TO SAINT BIRGITTA

"Then His eyes looked as if they were dim, His cheeks were
hollow, His mouth was open, His tongue bleeding, His stomach was flat against
His back, His whole body white from the great loss of blood.
His hands and feet were stretched out hard, and the
nails had made them, as it were, cross-shaped.
His beard and hair were full of blood."

✦

REV.VI.57

Leonhard Schäufelin, XVI C.   National Museum, Nuremberg

"MY GOD, MY GOD, WHY HAST THOU FORSAKEN ME?"

*"The princes of the world do not think now of making
pilgrimages to the places where I was born and suffered—instead they
now prefer to go to races. The prelates of the Church also like
worldly pleasures better than the contemplation
of My Passion and death."*

REV.VII.16

Avignon's Pietà, xv c.   *Louvre, Paris*

PIETÀ ACCORDING TO SAINT BIRGITTA

"The friends of the Lord took Him down from the Cross . . .
His hands were so stiffened that they could not be raised above the navel . . .
and His dolorous Mother took Him in her holy arms
and laid Him upon her knees . . .
and dried all His wounds with a linen cloth."

✦

REV. VII. 15

Biagio Puccini, XVIII C. *Domus Birgittae, Rome*

IN QUEST OF THE HOLY GRAIL

*Her mission accomplished, Birgitta died with
a gentle smile of a heroic woman who in her quest of the Holy
Grail fought a good fight and found her Redemption.*

Santa Rita Church   *Frascati near Rome*

RELIGIOUS INVESTITURE

*His Eminence Alfredo Cardinal Ottaviani,
the High Protector of the Order of Saint Birgitta, bestows the Cross
of Merit upon a noble lady of charity. The Order
supports several orphanages in Naples.*

Ecumenical dialogue   *Vatican City, 1966*

FOR THE CAUSE OF CHRIST AND UNITY

*His Holiness Pope Paul VI received the world famous
tenor Lauritz Melchior in a private audience. Lauritz, a prominent
Lutheran of Denmark, was honored with a Grand Cross of
Saint Birgitta in a religious-knightly
ceremony in Naples.*

Knightly ceremony   *St. Birgitta Church, Naples*

TRADITIONAL INVESTITURE

*"The Military Order of St. Birgitta was instituted by Princess Birgitta
of Sweden in 1366 under Pope Urban V, who approved the
Order by giving it the Augustinian Rule."*
*"The Order was reconstituted in 1859 and approved by King
Francis II of Naples and Sicily."*

-◇-

ENCYCLOPÉDIE CATHOLIQUE, 1842

FENICIA, MILIZIA SACRA, 1862

Chapter V

BOOK OF QUESTIONS

Book of Questions

The *Revelations* are divided into eight books with an appendix, the *Extravagantes*. "Words of God according to Birgitta" are presented in Book V, known as the "Book of Questions." In its original Latin version it consists of some sixteen thousand words; some authors consider it a moral and theological *Summa* by Saint Birgitta.

During her journey from the monastery of Alvastra to Vadstena, where she founded the first national monastery in Sweden, Birgitta had a vision of a ladder suspended between heaven and earth. A rather determined monk was climbing the ladder — as if storming heaven itself. Reminiscent of Job in the Old Testament, the monk tested the patience of the Lord the Judge with a series of questions. Birgitta could perceive that the monk cared more "to dispute than to live by the Gospels."

On her return, in the quiet of Alvastra, Birgitta recorded the conversation in the "Book of Questions." The condensed form which follows reflects the medieval spirit, but after six hundred years the subject matter is still contemporary. At the Council of Basel in 1434, the French Cardinal Johannes Gerson questioned the *Revelations* on matters of faith and doctrine. The Spanish Cardinal Johannes Torquemada defended them on theological grounds in one hundred and twenty-three accounts. Birgitta's legacy was assured by the Church.

Monk: Why have You given us feelings, if we can not use them freely at our own will?

Judge: My friend, man's feelings are not to be used just for a good diversion; they are created in him to serve the good of his soul.

Monk: Why is one not permitted to be proud, since Your Passion has forgiven us our sins? Why is it not permitted to revenge oneself?

Judge: Pride alienates man from heaven; humility leads to heaven. The role of the human body and the temporal pleasures is to acquire eternal good for man's soul. The source of justice is not vengeance but charity.

Monk: Why have we physical appetites which we are forbidden to satisfy? Why is food offered if we must not satiate ourselves? Of what use is our free will, if can not exercise it? The sex instinct if it must be denied? The heart, if we must repress its desires for enjoyment?

Judge: Man is endowed with intelligence to guide his appetites and emotions along the path of righteousness and to keep them from the path of self-destruction. Food supports and strengthens man's powers, but taken in excess, it exhausts them. The only sensible use of free will is to renounce one's own will and submit to the will of God. The union of man and woman has no other purpose than legitimate transmission of life. Man's heart is destined to contain My divinity; there has to be delight in Me.

Monk: Why should I seek divine wisdom when I am gifted with human wisdom? Why cry in despair when I swim in prosperity, and why delight in affliction of the flesh? Why fear when I am strong? Why submit my will, that of which I am the master?

Judge: The man who is wise according to the world is blind according to God; one must search humbly after the divine wisdom. Worldly honors lead man to his downfall if he does not accept them

73

with prayers and tears. On the contrary, affliction and infirmity of the flesh lead to inner happiness. Human strength is nothing compared to divine power. Free will deprived of divine guidance can be nothing but a source of license and sin.

MONK: Why do You allow disabilities, unequal courts of justice, the horror of death?

JUDGE: Disabilities strike the body, purifying the soul and subjugating it to patience. The inequity of judges, if not tolerated, leads to reform and the progress of justice. At the hour of death it is right that man purify himself by suffering.

MONK: Why do some children die before being born, though gifted with a soul, while others live to receive Baptism? Why do You permit the ruin of the just, and good fortune for the unbeliever? Why do we have plagues, hunger, unforeseen deaths and murder?

JUDGE: The child might die before being born either because of the sins of his parents, or because of My intervention for his soul. I treat the child with mercy even though he could not rejoice in the Beatific vision of My world. At times the just must suffer afflictions, which must be tolerated even without understanding the purpose; by believing, like the child becoming a man, they will see the reason for the discipline that has formed them. Tribulations save the unbelievers because an easy life would make them even more evil. Man endures plague and famine so that he who does not confess to Me in gratitude confesses to Me out of fear. If man knew the moment of his death, he would serve God out of fear instead of charity. And is it not just that man should be struck by unforeseen death, since he himself has digressed from certainty? As for murders, they are permitted to show the just man the damnation servants of Satan deserve.

MONK: Why are there beautiful and vile things in the world? Why should not I — one who is beautiful, rich and of noble blood — rise above the common people? Why shouldn't I be preferred over the others, for am I not worthy of more honors? Why shouldn't I aspire to the glory which I deserve?

JUDGE: The goods of this world are only good for those who despise them. Every man is conceived in inequity. His will can not change anything of the blood of which he is born. If the nobleman is superior to the commoner, the nobleman should fear that his ultimate Judgment will be more severe, because God has given him more. Besides, man only possesses what he has so that he may share it. To pride oneself in riches lent by Providence would be an usurpation; to expect praise but a delusion. Only God, the source of all creation and love, is praiseworthy. If man demands a worldly reward for his charity, he deprives himself of the eternal reward.

MONK: Why do You permit the worship of idols? Why not reveal Your glory to man so he will desire only You? Why not show him the angels, the saints, the demons and the eternal punishment?

JUDGE: By crushing the idols I would curb the freedom of man and make him unworthy of My justice. If I would appear to him in My glory surrounded by My heavenly host, he would long to die from mere joy. The saints reveal themselves under a veil of human infirmity, so that their beauty does not distract man from the worship of God. The sight of hell would leave man prey to a terror which would destroy his charity. Moreover, if he could behold the world beyond, where would be the merit of his faith, the fruit of his love?

MONK: Why the inequality of the divine gifts? Why has Mary been preferred above other beings? Why does the angel, the pure soul, live in gladness while man passes his existence in suffering? Why is reason given to the race of Adam and denied to the animals? Why does the light of day make way for the night?

JUDGE: The divine foreknowledge is not the cause of inequality of man. No one equals Mary in glory, because no one equals her in love. The revolt of some of the angels created before man's time introduced evil into the creation of the world. Among the angels, the haughty ones whom nothing excited to evil except the disorder of their own wills were punished without remission; the humble angels revel in God alone; their constancy assures them of paradise forever. The suffering endured by man in his world inspire his humility and enable him to merit eternal glory. Animals are denied reason, so that man can dominate them. The night invites rest, without which the indefatigable soul would break the body. Light represents the eternal day of the chosen and enables man to endure his afflictions; man's sins will deprive him of the lights of paradise. The darkness of the earth reminds him of his original sin.

MONK: Why has Your divinity been arrayed in human nature? How can it contain but not be contained? Why weren't You born right after the conception, with maturity of age? Being conceived without sin, why were You circumsized and baptized?

JUDGE: The manner of Redemption should be equal to the sin. The supernatural life lost by man's nature was returned to him by divine charity, when God became visible to man and sealed the reconciliation through love. Because God's divinity contains all things, nothing can contain it. I have assumed the human form and have grown like other children in order not to distract man's mind by a marvel that would inspire fear, not charity. I was circumsized even though only through My Virgin Mother was I of the race of Adam; otherwise, My enemies would have said, "He commands to do what He does not wish to do Himself." My Baptism is an example, and it indicated to man that heaven opens to him as it did to Me.

MONK: Why have You not revealed Your divinity with Your humanity? Why have You not at the same time revealed Your word and completed Your work, showing Your power at the instant of Your death?

JUDGE: At the sight of My divinity people would have been consumed and annihilated with joy. The prophets themselves have not contemplated the divine being. When I desired to show Myself to man, I took man's form. The full meaning of My word could not have been distributed all at once; it acts upon successive needs of the soul, as daily bread acts upon the constant needs of the body. Although time does not exist for Me, I established a succession of periods in My earthly life, as well as in the creation of the world. Together the believers and unbelievers surrounded Me. I had to uphold the faith of the faithful through teachings and tolerate My enemies. Had I revealed Myself to the people all at once, they would have followed Me not out of love, but fear, and the mystery of Redemption would not have been accomplished. According to the prophets, My innocent body was similar to the body that sinned in the form of Adam, so that I would be equal to those I came to redeem, so that I could work from morning till night, year after year, until My death. In that last hour I did not manifest My power, in order to fulfill the prophecies and to leave the example of patience. By descending the Cross I would not have enlightened the unbelievers, who were unmoved when I cured the sick and revived the dead. They would have attributed these miracles to man's magic instead of God's power.

MONK: Why were You born from a virgin? Why have You not revealed the virginity of Your mother by some obvious sign? Why did You make Your birth known only to a few? Why did You flee to Egypt and allow the massacre of innocents? Why did You endure the blasphemy that triumphed over truth and led to Your Crucifixion?

JUDGE: I was born from a virgin because virginity is the purest state of woman on earth. A miracle proving the virginity of My mother would not have convinced the unbelievers, who disregarded Joseph's testimony and the predictions of the prophets. I have left Mary the privacy of being unnoticed, and the humble character of My birth blends perfectly with that of man. I concealed the moment of My coming in this world so that the devil, My adversary, would not know it before the determined time, nor the people before the intended hour. My flight into Egypt was a manifestation of My disability as a man who must flee persecution for the greater glory of God. The massacre of the innocents was a form of My Passion and revealed the mystery of the divine call. I endured the blasphemers in expectation of their eventual conversion. It is not God, but man, preferring wrong over right, who allows blasphemy to rule.

MONK: Oh Judge, why do You pardon certain sinners and deny pardon to others? Why do You sometimes bestow the child with grace, then deny him in his old age? Why the inequalities of knowledge and understanding? Why pronounce some men right at the beginning and others at the end of their lives?

JUDGE: Intoxicated with liberty, man must learn that everything comes to him from God; thus pardon is sometimes granted, other times refused. God is able to foresee faithfulness in some children and their resistance of faith as old men. Faith in God ferments at the start of man's life, giving beneficial lights, later withdrawing them to prevent man's grace from increasing the severity of his Judgment. Often the unbeliever refuses to suffer without complaining; yet if he escapes suffering in this world, it is to be feared that he will be damned in the next. Knowledge and understanding are meaningless without the guiding spirit. Every man possesses the knowledge necessary to save himself. Sometimes only a small light enlightens; the more man's spirit would be dazzled and distracted by a larger one, the more he would be inclined to doubt. The man who abuses his reason will be punished. To write well and speak well is mere vanity if one does not live well. The extent of God's pardon corresponds to the use man makes of his free will. The prosperity of the wicked shows the patience of God. The adversity of the just testifies to the problems he must endure to prove the inconstancy of earthly joys. The hour of true vocation is when man hears the ultimate heavenly call to God.

MONK: Why do animals suffer, though they can not revel? Why, though they come into life without sin, must they endure pain? Why must the newly born, who is unaware of evil, be doomed to bear the responsibility of his father's mistakes? Why does the unexpected upset the anticipation? Why does the death of an unbeliever sometimes seem glorious, and that of a believer seem vile?

JUDGE: Animals are born in pain and sometimes live in affliction because the race of Adam caused all creation the ordeal of suffering for his original sin. Man, the author of evil, must bear it. The child is born bearing the sin of the father, for nothing of pure substance springs from man's being, although Baptism frees the Christian. Every man is free to ignore the fatal examples that perpetuate the punishments in his race, and since the Redemption, every man answers for his deeds alone. God conceals His plans for man in order to moderate His fear with love, and His love with fear. God is the source of life, of the prosperities and adversities which mark its course. Often earthly rewards precede the heavenly punishment, and for some, earthly punishment precedes the heavenly reward. The devil surrounds man with vain glory.

MONK: Why have You created useless things? Why can one not see souls? Why the undeserved diseases and pain? Judging from the liberties You give to the evildoers, why shouldn't one be as evil as he wants?

JUDGE: I have not created anything useless, but, by his original sin, man has deprived himself of seeing the true value of My creation. Just as the child brought up in darkness can not conceive the light of day, man can no more understand the heavenly lights. The soul is too superior to the body to be noticed by the bodily eyes. God does not always fulfill the prayers of His flock, for He sees better their real good. Heavenly justice removes, for a time, the unbelievers from the devil, endeavoring to return them to a state of grace, offering them the example of those believers whom trials incite to great undertakings. By passing through temptation, the faithful can understand the effectiveness of pardon, for, without true personal effort, they could never be saved. The soul of man preserves, because of his free will, the power to sin. If man's soul rejects God, then God leaves his soul. The devil is the executioner of the just, for whom his torment increases the eternal glory. He is also the executioner of the evil, whom he tortures, sometimes even in this life, though they die acclaimed.

MONK: Why do You have the sheep at Your right side and the goats at Your left? Why, if You are equal to God, has it been written that neither You nor the angels knew the hour of Judgment? Why is there disagreement in the accounts of the evangelists, when all four were inspired by the Holy Spirit? Why did You so long postpone Your Incarnation? Why, after having declared that saving a single soul is worth more to You than the world, have You sent Your preachers everywhere in the world?

JUDGE: The right and the left side of God can only be understood in the spiritual sense; these are light and darkness, the sublime glory and the privation of all good. The sheep and the goats symbolize innocence and sin. I did not know the hour of Judgment, hidden to all creatures, as a man — not as God. The Holy Spirit differs in His work and inspirations; the complete truth is found in the union of all Gospels; certain among them convey the letter, others the spirit of My lessons. My Incarnation arrived at its time, after natural law had revealed the inclination of humanity to good, and the written law had shown man human misery. Made in the image of My divinity, man is the noblest creature on earth. If he abuses his reason and My gifts, the time of My justice replaces that of My mercy; he is no longer worthy of listening to the message of Salvation.

Chapter VI

ORDER OF THE HOLY SAVIOUR

Order of the Holy Saviour

At the monastery of Alvastra, Christ revealed to Birgitta, "I will plant a new vineyard from which many other vineyards shall arise. And thou, Birgitta, shalt plant the young vines. Plant them in good places and shelter them against the cold and frost, against the heat and drought. Stand firm in your faith, and love Me with all thy heart. Flee from pride and live in humility." (Extrav. 73)

In humility Birgitta raised eight children; took care of hospitals, orphanages and monasteries; made arduous pilgrimages and advised King Magnus on behalf of justice. In obeying Christ's command to found the first national Religious Order of the Holy Saviour and to build a mother monastery at Vadstena, Birgitta made a total commitment.

On the shore of Lake Vättern at Vadstena, where a pagan temple once stood and human sacrifices were once offered, now the site of an abandoned castle of the Folkungs, the mother monastery was built. To redeem the shedding of innocent blood in the past and the iniquities of the present, Birgitta advised King Magnus to bestow the castle and the land for the future monastery. King Magnus, impressed by his prophetic cousin and interested in saving his own soul, followed her suit and even introduced a tax to support the monastery. But it was Birgitta, as the Process of Canonization ascertains, who gave up all riches, all honors at the court, her happiness among her children and even her country to further her monastery and the Order.

The Rule of the Order of the Holy Saviour was revealed to Birgitta by Christ. It states that there should be double monasteries chiefly for the nuns, *"per mulieres primo et principaliter,"* with thirteen priests, in memory of the Apostles including Saint Paul, four deacons and eight brothers. During her pilgrimage through France, Birgitta and her husband Prince Ulf became aware of double monasteries headed by an abbess. In memory of the Blessed Mother, the Queen of the Apostles on earth — according to the words of Christ on the Cross: "Behold thy Mother," the head of the Birgittine monastery would be an Abbess General. In the spiritual domain a Confessor General would serve as an adviser. The nuns would lead an ascetic and contemplative life of prayer and work, and the priests an active apostolic life. The convent for the nuns and the *curia* — house — for priests would be strictly separated by a *clausura*, and the monasteries would be under the jurisdiction of the bishop.

Every Birgittine monastery was dedicated to Mary; they were given names such as "Valley of Mary," "Mountain of Mary," and "Triumph of Mary." Birgitta's rosary with sixty-three *Ave Maria's*, in memory of Mary's years on earth, contributed to the popular devotion called *Marienminne.* Birgitta's vision of Mary's Assumption to Heaven (Rev. VI. 61), was proclaimed a dogma by Pope Pius XII in 1950. The Mariology was greatly enriched by Birgitta's *Sermo Angelicus* describing Mary's virtues. Even Martin Luther marveled at hundreds of thousands of pilgrims' chanting Birgitta's devotional prayers from one shrine to the next.

Medieval man's knightly and popular devotion to the Virgin Mary enhanced the respect of womanhood. Being born in the province of Uppland, where women were considered equal to men, Birgitta naturally envisioned a world in which a free and noble woman would be equal to a man before God and the law. Therefore, an abbess or a prioress would be a natural leader of a double monastery. Strindberg called Birgitta the first emancipated woman; Pope Pius XI considered her the symbol of the Catholic Women's Action.

The Vadstena monastery became a spiritual and cultural center of Sweden. Its monks excelled as theologians, bishops, historians, artists and writers. It housed a great library and its own printing facilities. The literary language of the Birgittine school could have become a common language of Scandinavia if politics had not intervened. The master edition of the *Revelations*, printed in 1492 in Lübeck, Germany, emerged second in popularity only to the Bible. Unfortunately, a few years later a fire at Vadstena destroyed much of the library, the printing house and the hospital.

Besides being a cultural center, Vadstena was a religious and social retreat for the Swedish aristocracy, as several queens and princesses entered the monastery. However, Vadstena could not escape the effects of the political turmoil and strife between the Kalmar-Unionists and the nationalists. The Kalmar Union of Norway, Sweden and Denmark was established by the great Queen Margareth of Denmark in 1396, the same year Birgitta was proclaimed patron saint of Sweden. A Swedish national hero, Engelbrecht, at the site of Birgitta's tomb called on his compatriots to rise against King Erik XIII of the Union. When King Christian II of Denmark later invaded Sweden, he executed some eighty noblemen at Stockholm's square, and the resulting revolution was unavoidable. King Christian II tried to appease the Swedes by making a pilgrimage of repentance to the tomb of Saint Birgitta, but Gustav Eriksson Vasa led a rebellion and liberated Sweden.

On his mother's side King Gustav I was related to Birgitta. Like Birger Earl in the thirteenth century, Gustav Vasa was an astute realist, interested in destroying the Kalmar Union and its supporters and securing Sweden's frontiers against Denmark. To achieve these goals he needed a full treasury, and the only way to obtain one was to secularize Church lands. To further justify this action Gustav I felt it necessary to change the Swedish religion to Lutheranism. No one dared to call the Liberator King Gustav I Vasa a heretic, and no Sir Thomas More came forth to stake his life for the principle. The break with Rome was definitive. Vadstena was looted of its riches; manuscripts and books were sequestered or burned; nuns were raped and some beheaded by the king's soldiers. A few Swedish monks and nuns escaped to Rome and Poland. Saint Birgitta's legacy in the history of Sweden was ended by Gustav Eriksson Vasa, her own distant blood relative.

If Gustav I and his successors had channeled their statesmanship into a Kalmar Union, a United States of Scandinavia with Stockholm as the capital might have been the result. Instead during the seventeenth century King Gustav II Adolphus shed Swedish blood all over Germany, fighting the Catholics in order to establish a mythical *Corpus Evangelicorum*, a Union of Protestant nations under the leadership of Sweden. In the eighteenth century King Charles XII, a romantic soldier, exhausted Sweden by fighting in Poland and Russia. Thus, the *Vasasaga*, begun by sacrificing spiritual and cultural progress for military glory came to an end.

The destruction of Birgitta's spiritual legacy at Vadstena uprooted the very Gothic soul of Sweden, and the resulting vacuum prevented new ideas from developing. The fifteenth-century Christian humanism in Vadstena normally would have evolved into a Renaissance and later a Baroque period as occurred in the rest of Europe. But Sweden was caught up in a conflict which revealed itself in Queen Christine. This intelligent, charming princess was raised with the Viking-like discipline and avenging wrath of her Protestant father, King Gustav II Adolphus. At the same time she rebelliously yearned for the mystical warmth of Catholicism; she collected the Renaissance art she missed in her own country, discussed philosophy and science with the great Descartes and, under the influence of a Spanish ambassador, dreamed of Southern Europe. She abdicated her throne, became a convert and theatrically descended upon Europe.

Most of Europe rejoiced in Queen Christine's conversion, which recalled the glory of Saint Birgitta. But Christine could not conceive that seventeenth-century Europe was undergoing a Catholic revival of piety after the fleshy heaviness of the Renaissance and the sobering experience of the Reformation. In Louvain a famous Jesuit hoped that Christine might be another Saint Birgitta, but Christine quipped, "rather a scholar than a saint." While in Rome at the Barberini palace, *A Glory of Saint Birgitta* was performed in Christine's honor, but the bored queen only yawned. If a cardinal and not the Pope himself served her Mass at Saint Peter's, she became angry, talking loud and playing with her little dog. To the great embarrassment of the Church she allowed her intimate adviser to be killed in front of her eyes. Europe and even sophisticated France shuddered. A Birgittine "Seer of Lyons" thundered in protest that Christine's art collection of nude nymphs and goddesses was pornographic; he denied that she could have descended from the country of Saint Birgitta. The aging Christine eventually resigned herself to the fashionable cult of Quietism. Lamenting over her lost youth, she died among her paintings. To the surprise of Europe the all-forgiving Church allowed her to be buried in Saint Peter's opposite Michelangelo's Pietà.

From the mother monastery at Vadstena, the young vines had been planted in good places, and the daughter monasteries in Finland, England, Germany and Italy made a lasting impact on Europe.

Even during the early Renaissance, Nuremberg and Florence were the commercial and cultural centers of Europe. Florentine merchants and bankers loved life with a Southern passion, but they cherished culture also. Florentine leading families such as Acciaiuoli, Buondelmonti, Soderini, Alberti and Medici either met Birgitta in Rome or knew of her apostolate in Italy. Even before she was canonized, Birgitta's *Revelations*, brought to Florence by her confessor Bishop Alphonse of Jaen, were the topic of discussions led by Marsilius at the fashionable salon *Santo Spirito* and by Antonio degli Alberti at the *Paradiso.* Bishop Alphonse was no stranger to the Florentines, because he had mediated the peace between Pope Gregory XI and Florence. In Pisa, Bishop Alphonse met Chiara Gambacorta, a future saint, who saw Saint Birgitta as her advocate with God. Chiara, the daughter of the most influential family in Pisa, arranged public sermons on Birgitta's *Revelations* and her saintly virtues. At this point Antonio degli Alberti, a rich merchant, humanist and poet, decided to bestow his *Paradiso* estate to be converted into a monastery of Saint Birgitta.

Pope Boniface IX, who had recently canonized Birgitta, accepted Alberti's gift, and the Archbishop Corsini consecrated the grounds and the buildings. Alberti's three daughters entered the convent. Another Christian humanist, Petrus ser Mini, whose friend Chancellor Salutati dominated the intellectual life of Florence, entered the monastery. Mini's three brothers faithfully followed him. The "Paradise of S. Mary and S. Birgitta" became a center of piety, charity and culture in Florence. Unfortunately, a feud broke out between the powerful families of Albizzi and Alberti, and Antonio degli Alberti found himself a financially ruined refugee in Rome. The propapal city authorities took the monastery under their protection.

The practical merchants and bankers of Florence were impressed by Birgitta's mysticism because it was neither morose nor emotionally exalted, but a concrete dialogue of love and devotion to Christ. Such a mysticism gave them reassurance in facing the fluctuations of success and failure in their lives. In 1415, the young banker Cosimo Medici escorted Pope John XXIII (later antipope) to the ecumenical Council of Constance, which was opened by exalting Saint Birgitta. Cosimo Medici, the Archbishop Antoninus — himself a future saint — and the authorities of Florence proclaimed in the *Provvisioni No. 128* that July twenty-third would be a holiday in honor of Saint Birgitta.

When the Council of Ferrara became endangered by the pestilence and by lack of funds, Cosimo Medici, as a friend and the banker of the ecumenical Pope Eugene IV, offered to bear the expense of a Council meeting to be held in Florence. During the Council, Cosimo must have listened with great satisfaction as the Greeks declared, "We recognize that the Pope is the sovereign pontiff . . . the representative and Vicar of Christ; that he rules and governs the Church of God . . . " It sounded as if they were reading Birgitta's *Revelations.* (VII. 19) No wonder, when the leaders of the Council of Florence in 1439 were Cardinal-statesmen like Albergatti, Cesarini, Torquemada and Orsini, who had already fought the battle for Birgitta at the Council of Basel. Before Cosimo died, he built the famous San Marco monastery. Grateful Florentines proclaimed Cosimo Medici "Father of the Fatherland," not because of his wealth, but because he used it to the glory of God and Florence.

According to popular tradition, Birgitta on her pilgrimage from Sweden to Rome in 1349 passed through the Republic of Genoa. Birgitta's confessor, Bishop Alphonse of Jaen, ended his lifelong apostolate by founding the Monastery of Saint Jerome for the hermits in Quarto, near Genoa. He brought with him the original copy of Birgitta's *Revelations*, which fascinated the elite of the city. Birgitta had hardly been canonized when a powerful Confraternity of Saint Birgitta came into existence. During the French occupation of Genoa the governor Marschal Jean Boucicaut showed great devotion to Saint Birgitta and great charity toward the city. Once the Birgittine monastery was built in Florence, the Confraternity requested a daughter monastery to be built in the scenic hills of Quarto. Under the apostolate of Johannes ser Mini, brother of Petrus, several brothers from Florence moved to the monastery of the "Heavenly Path of Mary and Birgitta." The angelic monastery became the spiritual center of Genoa; as Cnattingius writes, "more souls had been led to God through this monastery than by all the other monasteries in the town . . . the monastery reached such a degree of piety and holiness that it stood out like a great shining light in the town of Genoa, to the glory of God and the good repute of the Birgittine Order." In the same quarter of the city, Quarto, Christopher Columbus was born. According to the Spanish historian Jimenez, Columbus often climbed the steep path to the monastery while reciting the "Glories of Our Lady" and the "Passion of Our Lord." Before leaving for the New World, Columbus stayed in a Birgittine hospice in Murcia, and it is not an accident that his flagship was named *Santa Maria*, and the first land he sighted, *San Salvador*, the Holy Saviour.

Brother Johannes ser Mini refused to admit nuns into the monastery of the "Heavenly Path." This decision, made in good faith and approved by Archbishop Pileo Marini and the city fathers of Genoa, brought the whole concept of Birgittine monasticism into question. According to the Rules approved by Pope Urban V in 1370 in the

Bull *Hiis quae divini,* the monastery should consist of two convents, one for the nuns and one for the priests. The term convent legally implies a religious corporation. Even in Vadstena, the mother monastery, not a convent, but only a *curia* existed for the priests. Renaissance Italy could not conceive of a monastery for both nuns and monks, even though they would be strictly separated by the *clausura.* Once the issue was raised, it became a legal and constitutional problem with almost catastrophic consequences for the Order.

The fifteenth century witnessed the Birgittine monasteries flourishing like "the young vines." The controversy over single and double monasteries arose in Genoa and reached its full momentum with the Syon Abbey in England. The problem can be understood only in perspective of the changing times — the Middle Ages evolving into a new age.

At the ecumenical Council of Constance Pope John XXIII solemnly reconfirmed the canonization and the double monasteries of Saint Birgitta. The first who pledged to build a magnificent monastery, "Triumph of Mary," were the Poles, who in their victory over the Teutonic Order at Tannenberg saw fulfillment of Birgitta's prophecy. (Rev. VIII. 31) After his victory at Agincourt in 1415, King Henry V of England married the French princess, as Birgitta had indicated in her *Revelations,* IV. 105. As a thanksgiving, King Henry bestowed his royal estate at Syon outside of London for the double monastery of the "Immaculate Conception and Birgitta." Shakespeare portrayed Henry V saying, "I have built two chantries, where sad and solemn priests still sing for Richard's soul," referring to King Henry's atonement for the imprisonment and death of King Richard II. The Birgittine monastery at Syon became a spiritual center of fifteenth-century England, and the Cult of Saint Birgitta remained strong even through the religious persecutions held during the reigns of King Henry VIII and Queen Elizabeth I. A martyred Birgittine monk, Richard Reynolds, was canonized in 1970.

The Schism ended at the Council of Constance, and Pope Martin V confirmed previous bulls concerning the double monasteries. But later, to the great surprise of the kings, princes and the Birgittines, Pope Martin, influenced by changing times in Italy, reversed himself and favored single monasteries. King Henry V, King Erik XIII and Emperor Sigismund, the High Protector of the Birgittines, insisted on another reversal. Finally Thomas Fishbourne, Confessor General of the Syon Abbey, a once wealthy landowner who dedicated his life to Saint Birgitta, undertook a mission to Rome. Through his relative, Bishop Clifford of London, and his friend Herman Dwerg, the most influential Englishman at the Curia, Fishbourne approached the two greatest canonists of the Middle Ages, Cardinal Tudeschi-Panormitanus and Dominic of San Gimignano, and requested their legal opinions. Under canon law double monasteries were forbidden; however, the two prestigious men's opinions agreed with Saint Birgitta's intent: that the monastery would consist of one convent for the nuns — a collegium — and only a house — a curia — for the priests. Pope Martin V in his Bull *Excellentium principum* accepted this interpretation and regained the favor of the Northern countries. Birgittine monasteries flourished in England, Poland, Germany, Holland, the Baltic lands and Scandinavia. Gifts and donations from the landed aristocracy — mostly husbands and wives, brothers and sisters entering the monasteries — supported them. In Italy, however, because of the conflicting definitions, the single and the double monasteries eliminated each other. Growing Protestantism in the North caused the Birgittine monasteries, except in Finland, to be abolished. Only in the seventeenth century during the Catholic revival did the monasteries start to flourish again.

When King Henry V built the monastery at Syon in 1415, his brother-in-law, King Erik XIII of the Kalmar Union, converted Grimstorp Castle in Loland, Denmark into "Maribo" monastery. Another, "Maria Ager," was built in the province of Jutland. A devotee of Saint Birgitta following in the footsteps of his adoptive mother Queen Margareth, King Erik also envisioned the Birgittine monasteries as spiritual bridges unifying Scandinavia, but conflicting interests between Denmark and Sweden broke the axis of the Kalmar Union.

Both Queen Margareth and Erik's wife Queen Philippa, in accord with their wishes, were buried close to Saint Birgitta at Vadstena.

In the territory of the Teutonic Order in Estonia, a large monastery, "Mariental," was founded in Reval by Grand Master Konrad von Vietinghof. Birgitta in her writings often admonished the Teutonic Knights not to neglect their monastic virtues. In Poland, King Ladislaus II established a great national shrine and monastery, "Triumph of Mary," in honor of Saint Birgitta. In Norway, in memory of the pilgrimage by Prince Ulf and Birgitta to the shrine of Saint Olaf, the Hansa town of Bergen built a monastery, "Munkaliv," as a center of piety and culture.

A chain of monasteries was erected along the Northern German and Dutch coasts in the fifteenth century. Two rich Hansa towns, Stralsund and Lübeck, established the monasteries "Marienkron" and "Mariawohlde" through donations of land by aristocracy and funds by local merchants. The most important German monastery, "Gnadenburg," near Nuremberg, was founded by Princess Catherine, sister of King Erik XIII. Although Catherine once lived at Vadstena, she preferred "Paradiso" in Florence as a prototype monastery. Both the Lübeck and Nuremberg monasteries were under the Emperor's protection. Nuremberg compared to Florence as a cultural center, and Renaissance life in Germany could not be imagined without the influence of Birgitta and her *Revelations.*

At the turn of the fifteenth century, Emperor Maximilian, "the last knight," sponsored a large monastery at Altomünster. According to the story, Birgitta on her pilgrimage to Rome had bought the land and bestowed it to the town. A Birgittine prior of "Altomünster" who had fallen away from the Church at the beginning of the Reformation marveled about the simplicity of one of his monks: "I am calling you happy because your simple faith will lead you to heaven, while my vain knowledge will take me to hell." Even today one can see Birgitta's pilgrim staff and bowl among the curios of the monastery.

From another South German monastery, "Maria Maihingen," near Öttingen the Rhine River flows past "Marienforst" at Godesberg and "Marienbaum" at Cleve. From "Marienkamp" monastery at Kampen several monasteries branch out to "Mariensterre" in Gouda, about which Erasmus wrote with enthusiasm to Sir Thomas More. "Marienstern" in Essig, "Maria Wijngaard" in Utrecht and "Marienburg" in Soest, "Marienthron" in Termonde and "Maria Ager" in Brielle and "Marienwater" in Rosmalen were established by the Dukes of Burgundy and the Dukes of Brabant in cooperation with the merchants of the towns.

In seventeenth-century Spain a heroic woman, Blessed Marina de Escobar, became acquainted with the virtues and *Revelations* of Saint Birgitta. Although crippled for life, Blessed Marina directed all her energies to reconstituting the Birgittine Order of Recollection in the spirit of modern times. Advised by Jesuit Louis de la Ponte, she founded five monasteries in Spain and four more in Mexico. In Valenciennes and Arras Birgittine monasteries were established; many of the nuns met martyrs' deaths during the French Revolution. In Belgium in the nineteenth century a men's order, *Fratres Novissimi Birgittini*, was founded.

In the twentieth century a Swedish convert, Elizabeth Hesselblad, expanded the Birgittine Order to Iver Heath, England; Lugano, Switzerland; Djursholm, Sweden; Calcutta, India; and Darien, Connecticut in the United States. "Vikingsborg" in Darien is an ideal retreat for New York's business people and the United Nations diplomats. During her apostolate Reverend Mother Elizabeth was advised by Jesuit Enrico Rosa of *Civiltà Cattolica*. Her crowning success was in restoring to the Order the *Domus Birgittae* in Rome and returning the Birgittines to Vadstena, Sweden, after a three-hundred-year absence. Birgitta might become, as Cardinal Tisserant said, "an ecumenical bridge between Rome and Sweden." Today the Order is witnessing an expansion under the leadership of Abbess General Hilaria Laubenberger in Rome. And so the words of Christ, "and thou, Birgitta, shalt plant the young vines," have come true.

Chapter VII

KNIGHTHOOD OF SAINT BIRGITTA

Knighthood of Saint Birgitta

Knighthood has always implied elevation of the spirit over material values of life. The Roman *miles* was a man of civil and military virtues; the Chinese *kinn'tse* were men who cultivated virtues; in Japan they called them *Samurai.* In Byzantium knights cultivated literature and the arts, and in Arabia, a sophisticated way of life which influenced medieval Europe.

The barbarians who overran the Roman Empire were heathens and warriors, even after on the surface accepting Christianity. Their primitive code of honor and loyalty was limited to their chieftain and feudal locality. Another code existed in Europe at the same time — the code of Christianity, which insisted on peace and the brotherhood of man under God. The blending of the warrior ethos with the new Christian spirit created a new type of man, a knight. The Crusades gave Christian knighthood its character, when warrior energies were channeled toward the Holy Land with the goal of redeeming the Holy Sepulchre from the hands of the infidels. Local particularism was replaced with the universalism of Christianity, although with Christian knighthood there were certain specific religious-military orders such as the Knights of Saint John, known as the Order of Malta; the Knights of the Templars; the Knights of Saint Mary, known as the Teutonic Order; and the Knights of the Holy Sepulchre, who took both monastic and military vows. These orders of knighthood were exempt from local sovereignty and taxation and formed institutions in themselves. They were international in character like the Church itself.

These great religious-military orders groomed ascetics and warriors in a true medieval fashion. But the difference persisted between this "heavenly chivalry" and the secular chivalry. In Southern France, influenced by the Arabs during the Crusades, troubadours introduced the cults of worldly love and courtesy in a subtle and sophisticated way which greatly fascinated the rough warriors of Europe. However, the hedonism of secular chivalry was the antithesis of Saint Bernard's heavenly chivalry, and a conflict was inevitable. The secular and courtly culture of the troubadours lost its battle with the Northern European religious-military chivalry because it was more Spartan in discipline and more purposeful in faith.

But once Europe had tasted the pleasures of the world, secularization never stopped, regardless of its defeat in Provence and regardless of the horrors of the Black Death, which was supposed to bring Europe to her senses. The end of the Crusades in the Holy Land, the increasing wealth and luxury of Western Europe and the blossoming Renaissance all transformed the former knight into a charming courtier. But the ideal of Christian chivalry, dedication to God and His Church and the virtues on this earth, never lost its appeal to Western man.

Except for Saint Bernard, no saint exceeded Birgitta in writing on Christian chivalry as opposed to secular chivalry, which she used to call "the chivalry of the devil." The reasons for Saint Birgitta's awareness of knighthood are many. Both her parents were related to the royal families which introduced chivalry, particularly the Order of Seraphim, into Sweden. Her father was a Knight of the Sword, the order which fought in the Baltics against the barbarians; her husband was a Knight of the Golden Griffin; and her son Sir Birger was a Knight of the Holy Sepulchre. Saint Birgitta was deeply impressed with the Knights of Saint James of Compostella. She always stayed at the hospices of the Knights of Saint John during her pilgrimages. She admired the work of the Knights of Saint Lazarus, dedicated to the care of lepers. Her special love went to the Knights of Saint Mary, also

95

known as the Teutonic Order, who fought for the conversion of North-eastern Europe. As Christ revealed to Birgitta, "A knight who keeps the rules of his order is exceedingly dear to Me. For if it is hard for a monk to wear his heavy garb, it is still harder for a knight to wear his heavy armor." (Processus, 627b)

Because of such an awareness Birgitta wrote some hundred pages about knighthood, its structure, purpose, attire and ceremony. A knightly investiture according to Saint Birgitta is a case in point: "The brillant procession is moving on its way to the church, the king's banner waving at the head. But at the churchyard gate the procession stops; the gentlemen dismount and tether their horses at the fence; then they approach the church. Here they are met by the clergy in white capes, with candles and incense and the processional cross at the head. They all go into the church, each one to his place, and the Mass begins. But when the Mass has come to *Agnus Dei* — that is, just before the Communion — the man who is to be honored steps before the altar and the king asks him, 'Will you be a knight?' 'I will!' 'Do you promise God and me that you will defend the faith of the Holy Church and obey the bishops in all that belongs to God?' 'I promise.' Then the king gives him the sword and says, 'Behold, I give you this sword so that you may defend the faith and the Holy Church, defend God's friends and subdue His enemies.' Next the king gives him the shield and says, 'Behold, I give you this shield, so that you may protect yourself with it against God's enemies and protect the widows and orphans.' Then the king lays his hand upon the man's neck and says, 'Behold, I lay upon you the yoke of obedience. Fulfill by your deeds what you have promised.' The new knight is then clothed with the cape of knighthood, after which the Mass is continued and the priest gives the new knight Holy Communion." In spirit Birgitta hears the words of Christ to His new warrior. "I will be in him, and he shall be in Me. I will kindle in him the fire of My love, so that he shall will nought but what I will, and fear none other than Me. And I will be with him wherever he goes." (Rev. II. 13)

The failure of the Crusades of her cousin King Magnus Eriksson in Finland and the growing vanity of the Teutonic Knights made Birgitta very critical of secular chivalry, or rather, Christian chivalry which had become secularized. Referring to her once favorite Teutonic Order, she lamented, "The Lord revealed to me that He loved you above all other orders, for you swore to shed your blood for His. Once your very name instilled one with awe, and your knightly armor signified your self-denial and the strength of your faith. You were fortified against all weaknesses by obedience to your Rules, and because you did not rely on your own will, but on God's mercy. But now, alas, you do not follow Christ, your generous Master and the Knight Who entered Jerusalem to engage in a heroic and desperate battle for you. You do not sacrifice your life for truth and justice anymore, but enrich yourselves through cupidity and unjust wars. In doing so, you are inviting eternal wrath on your souls and closing the gate of heaven." (Rev. II. 7) Birgitta's warnings against the decadence of Christian knighthood are masterpieces of medieval literature. Birgitta envisioned the knight without blemish or reproach: "A knight of honor who strives with all his might to glorify God, and who is ready to suffer for God's sake what God wills that he should suffer, is God's knight and will be made a knight in heaven." (Rev. IV. 55) Because of her definite stand on knighthood Birgitta is considered a patroness of all knightly orders.

French historian Hermant in his volume, *The History of the Orders of Chivalry*, speaks with authority about the Birgittine chivalric order during the times when barbarians invaded Poland, Sweden, Denmark and the Baltic lands. Hermant says that Saint Birgitta instituted a military order in 1366 with the purpose of combating the invasion of the heathens, to limit the heretics in their expansion, and to take care of widows, orphans and the aged. The Knights of the Order of Saint Birgitta selected as an emblem a blue Maltese cross with a symbolic fire underneath it. The blue cross stood for the immense love of the Church, and the fire symbolized the ardor of the faith. The Order of Saint Birgitta was based on the Augustinian Rule and recognized by Pope Urban V in 1370. The standard of the Order has a cross on one side and three Gothic crowns on the other. Another prominent historian, Joseph Michele y Marquez, in Cavalleria Antiqua e Moderna, adds that the forms of arming the knights, the benedictions and the profession of the knights followed the pontifical of the Order of Saint John, known today as the Order of the Knights of Malta. The knights advanced according to seniority, giving young knights the opportunity eventually to become Grand Master of the Order. The Order persisted in Sweden until the Protestant revolution of 1559 and then moved out of the country into Poland, Germany, France, Spain and Italy. Historians such as Giustiniano in his work Ordini Militari e Cavallereschi, and Buonani in his Ordini Religiosi e Militari write in the same tradition about the Birgittine Order as do the prestigious Dizionario Storico-Ecclesiastico by Moroni and Dictionnaire des Dictionnaires in Paris.

Dahlberg, in his Suecia Antiqua e Moderna, speaks of the Knights of the Order of Saint Birgitta in Sweden about 1396. The time coincides with the establishment of the Kalmar Union between Norway, Sweden and Denmark by Queen Margareth and the proclamation of Saint Birgitta as patron saint of Sweden. Saint Olaf of Norway and Saint Birgitta of Sweden were envisioned as religious and spiritual guides for the unification of Scandinavia.

The book of the Swedish orders, Sweriges Riddarordnar of 1948, writes of the Chivalry of Saint Birgitta, *Riddare av S:ta Brita*, furnished with rich commenda by Queen Margareth at the monastery of Vadstena: "Ordo S:tae Birgittae, så kallad av den namnkunniga abedissan i Vadstena S:t Brita, blev utgiven av drottning Margareta 1396 och bar till tecken ett blått åttkantigt kors, av vars ena udd en glödande tunga utgick, som betydde S:t Britas syner och underverk. Stathallare Måns Påvelsson Bjugg var riddare av denna orden." King Erik XIII, Governor Benedict Magnusson of Ost-Gothland, Governor Birger Pettersson of Tiunda and thirty-six other knights were invested at the Church of Our Lady of Vadstena. It appears clearly that Queen Margareth bestowed Saint Birgitta's cross, *Vadstenatecknet*, as a royal decoration of merit.

Historian Bång in his Ulfspårre Ätten cites the names of Påvel Månsson Bjugg, Måns Påvelsson Bjugg and Abraham Påvelsson Bjugg, who received the knighthood of Saint Birgitta in 1447 for their generous assistance to the monastery of Vadstena. Mechtild Påvelsdotter was an Abbess General of the monastery. Several daughters of the family of Ulfspårre, distantly related to Saint Birgitta, joined the monastery. Lady Ingeborg Pettersson and Brita Månsdotter were invested as ladies of the Order. Many knights and ladies supported the Vadstena monastery generously. In the eighteenth century Queen Lovise Ulrika and Queen Ulrike Eleonora fashioned their decorations of merit according to Birgitta's cross, *Vadstenatecknet*.

The great fourteenth-century French poetess Christine de Pisan speaks of a well-known troubadour, Othon F. Guillaume, who in 1397, claimed that his literary fame disappeared before his glory as a brilliant Knight of the Holy Saviour, popularly known as the Order of Saint Birgitta. A. G. Horn, in his historical sketch on knightly orders, speaks in 1768 about the Knightly Order of Saint Birgitta for the Swedish Catholic aristocracy. In the Appendix, Article VII, he says at that time the Abbess General of the Birgittines in Rome was functioning as Grand Master of the Order.

In the nineteenth century encroaching liberalism — with its atheistic and secular overtones — threatened to destroy the Church, just as in the fourteenth century expanding pagan humanism tried to undermine Christianity. But in 1366, when Europe, according to a popular belief, expected the birth of Lucifer, Birgitta's Order of the Holy Saviour was born. Similarly in the nineteenth century the Southern Italian aristocracy, following their forefathers who had feted Birgitta in Naples, arose to the defense of the Church by reviving the traditional Knightly Order of Saint Birgitta. Some one hundred princely families of Southern Italy and others from Florence, Genoa, Bologna and Rome convened in three consecutive assemblies in the Church of the Holy Saviour in Capua near Naples, to reconstitute the Order. Among the leading families present were the Commenos, Pierangelis, Pignatellis, Caraffas, Paternos, Caracciolos and San Severinos. With the advice of the noble Cardinal Giuseppe de Cosenza and with approval of the chivalric King Francis II Bourbon of Naples and Sicily, the Order of the Holy Saviour and Saint Birgitta saw a new light. Naples, being at that time the largest city in Italy and the capital of the Kingdom of Both Sicilies, lent a great deal of prestige to the Order. C. Fenicia in his work Milizia Sacra di S. Birgitta, gives a complete picture of the reconstitution of the Order in 1859 under the hereditary Grand Mastership of Count Vincenzo Abbate de Castello Orléans.

When the House of Savoy came to the throne in 1861, many orders existing in the time of the Bourbons were abolished; and when the Republic of Italy was proclaimed in 1946, replacing the Savoys, again many orders were dissolved, but the Knights of the Order of Saint Birgitta survived. In 1959, one hundred years after the reconstitution of the Order, the Supreme Court of Italy declared it a "non-national and independent order." It is neither an ecclesiastical nor a state order, but a *de facto* link between Church and State. The present Grand Master of the Order is Count Vincenzo Abbate de Castello Orléans, Jr. The administrative seat of the Order is Naples, Italy.

Today's Order of the Knights of Saint Birgitta is following in the footsteps of the traditional *Equites Briccianes*, taking care of charities such as orphanages and monasteries, furthering Christian art, music and literature and expanding the ecumenical movement toward Christian unity. Today the Order is numerically one of the strongest in the world and, because of its ecumenical tendencies, the most contemporary. The strength of the Order is displayed in Italy, Spain, and Latin America, and it is the only order expanding in Africa. A special spiritual stronghold is located in Los Angeles, California, where the Ecumenical Foundation of America, based on the ideals of Saint Birgitta, was founded.

In these trying times, when the Church is in dangers similar to those of the fourteenth and nineteenth centuries, the Knights of the Order of Saint Birgitta are trying to answer the challenges of their time in defense of the Church and for the greater glory of God.

Epilogue

Epilogue

For all his study modern man can not define Birgitta's genius. Birgitta urged Pope Clement VI to proclaim the Holy Year; she advised King Magnus on his Crusade in Finland and intervened in behalf of peace during the Hundred Years' War, yet no explanation of the popes' and kings' compliance with the Sibyl of the North is possible. Heiler named Birgitta "the most remarkable woman in history." Gisbert Kranz begins his two-thousand-page master work, *Political Saints*, with Saint Birgitta; then Saint Bernard, Saint Francis, Saint Dominic, Saint Ignatius and many others follow. Birgitta's political theory was, "The world would have peace if the men of politics would only follow the Gospel."

Birgitta's legacy was defended by popes and kings; popes Urban VI; Martin V and Eugene IV; emperors Charles IV, Sigismund and Maximilian the First; Queen Margareth and kings Henry V and Erik XIII. Yet Birgitta often reproached popes and kings for not living in accordance with Christ's commands; as Nilsson in *History of Sweden* says, "Birgitta was of an indomitable spirit . . . to whom it came naturally to speak and write the truth to the princes of State and Church." The aristocracy and merchants competed to build her monasteries from Finland, Germany, England to Spain and Italy. Naples, Brussels and Vienna had whole quarters named after Birgitta.

During the Renaissance when Boccaccio's *Decameron* and Lorenzo Valla's *De Voluptate* — two "bibles of pleasure" — were drowning the Christian spirit, artists in Florence, Nuremberg and the Low Lands patiently worked on religious art according to Birgitta's *Revelations*. Even if daily life appeared to be "man-centered," artistic life persisted to be God-centered. In the final analysis Birgitta prevailed over Boccaccio, as the subsequent Baroque style proved. And during the religious persecutions in sixteenth-century Europe, Birgitta's devotional prayers, such as those in chapters III and IV, greatly comforted the unfortunates. During the Catholic revivals in seventeenth and nineteenth-century Europe, piety spread with the guidance of Birgitta's *Revelations* and devotions.

Birgitta's prophecies, such as those concerning the Black Death engulfing Sweden, the end of the Folkungs, the return of the Pope from Avignon, peace between the Pope and Emperor, the end of the Hundred Years' War, the fall of the Byzantine Empire, the Schism within the Church, the Vatican as a sovereign state and future Christian unity, kept Europe in expectation. Nostradamus in his master work of prophecies with great reverence dedicates several pages to Saint Birgitta. Her most recently fulfilled prophecy was the signing of the Lateran Treaty of 1929, which established the Vatican as a sovereign state. The daughter of the late dictator of Italy recently observed to this author, "My father signed the fulfillment of Birgitta's prophecy." But only God in His Infinite Wisdom knows when Birgitta's last prophecy, "The time will come when there shall be one flock and One Shepherd, one faith and one clear knowledge of God," (Rev. VI. 77) will be fulfilled. Christ's promise to Birgitta, "It shalt be through you that I will speak to the world," came true; the Holy Spirit with a tongue of fire spoke through Birgitta. Her *Vadstenatecknet* has a symbolic tongue of fire underneath it.

And Birgitta's tongue of fire spoke in many languages. The year 1534 is an important date in the spiritual history of Europe. Sir Thomas More, rather than profit the world by losing his soul, preferred martyrdom in the Tower of London. Through his friendship with the Birgittine monk Whitford, Sir Thomas became a diligent reader of the *Revelations*. Only a short time before his own death, Sir Thomas More observed another Birgittine monk, Blessed Richard Reynolds, also a friend, walking with a gentle smile to the scaffold. To Sir Thomas the rope around Reynolds' neck appeared as a golden chain of knighthood. Sir Thomas More's resoluteness to die for his faith has some origin in Saint Birgitta's definitiveness. There is something very personal, almost intimate, but always definitive about Birgitta's influence on great leaders in all walks of life. Until the end of the nineteenth century she was considered a patroness of the Christian nobility; today she is considered patroness of the Christian leadership, no longer of blood, but of spirit and of service to God.

Also in 1534, Saint Ignatius of Loyola founded the Society of Jesus. Saint Ignatius took his last vow in front of the "Cross of Saint Birgitta" at Saint Paul's Basilica in Rome. Ignatius accepted the proposal of his faithful Peter Canisius, devotee of Saint Birgitta, to influence the leadership of Austria and Germany to regain the ground lost during the Reformation. The Jesuit Order found princes in the Rhineland and Southern Germany quite receptive because the Birgittine influence was well-entrenched. Still in the same year Filippo Neri started his apostolate in Rome following the tradition of Saint Birgitta. Just as Birgitta through her visions in the Holy Land introduced the new style in the art of the Nativity and the Passion of Christ, Neri is responsible for the Oratorium Music developed by Palestrina, Bach, Handel and Haydn. Birgitta and Neri are often found on opposite sides of the same commemorative medal. And, finally, in the same year Pope Paul III came to the papal throne to convene the Council of Trent and reform the Church, as Birgitta had pleaded two hundred years earlier.

Birgitta's influence led to some stormy incidents in the history of Europe. Warrior Saint Joan of Arc, aware of Birgitta's prophetic powers, inspired France with the same zeal as Birgitta did Europe. Joan was burned at the stake. Savonarola thundered out of the San Marco monastery using the language and zeal of Saint Birgitta against the Medici family and the Roman Curia. Savonarola was burned at the stake. The "Holy Maid of Kent," a self-proclaimed "Birgittine prophetess," attacked King Henry VIII for his divorce, accursing him to the eternal fire of hell. She was also burned at the stake. Margery Kempe, anchoress of Lynn, believed she was a reincarnation of Birgitta and drove England, Europe and the Holy Land mad with her spells of overzealousness. Master Tortsch published Onus Mundi, reproaches and criticism of the Roman Curia attributed to Saint Birgitta. It was very fashionable to print all kinds of letters, pamphlets and even prayers attributed to Birgitta. Flacius, as the right hand of Luther, tried to explain Birgitta as a predecessor of Protestantism. Finally, the "Seer of Lyons," another self-proclaimed "Birgittine prophet," attacked Queen Christine for exhibiting her art collection of Renaissance nudes, nymphs and goddesses. Some Swedes today try to justify their trend of nudity and pornography as a sort of Renaissance. But many great Swedes honor Birgitta: Stiernhielm, father of Swedish poetry; Swedenborg, a great mystic; Tegner, a religious poet with a touch of the prophet; Heidenstam, a noble man of Swedish tradition; Selma Lagerlöf, a gentle soul almost praying for her Sweden; Lindblom, a devotee of Saint Birgitta; Cornell, who put Birgitta's influence on art into the right perspective; and Stolpe, who brought her back to the Swedish people through his prolific writings. Sweden indeed has experienced a strange metamorphosis from Viking paganism to Birgittine Catholicism, institutional Protestantism, empty churches and to spiritual vacuum. No nation can deny its patron saint forever. The spiritual vacuum is waiting for a renewal of the original source of Sweden's strength: Saint Birgitta.

Birgitta blessed the world with more than her prophecies. Above all, her personal philosophy made her a shining example for posterity. Birgitta took definitive stands on many facets of life: For a woman's equality to man before God and the law. For adoration of Mary as the most loving mother, who can serve any woman as an example. Against abortions, because no man has the right to destroy the mystery of God's creation. That the dignity of human life must be preserved. Against fashions which thrill the fancy and entice the flesh. Against the marriage of priests, who should with their purity shine before the faithful as light in darkness. For obedience to the Vicar of Christ, as Christ Himself was obedient to His Father until death. That the army of Christ can not march forward except under one supreme command. Against slavery because all humans are children of God. That government should preserve the rights of the individual.

Neither her prophecies nor her positions taken on vital issues disclose the very soul of Saint Birgitta. Her life energies — pulsating with love, devotion and absolute obedience to Christ — transformed this Viking warrior woman into a great Christian heroine. Her rich experiences with the courts and princes, who appeared outwardly so alive yet through their sins were already spiritually dead, made Birgitta realize that sin was the only real death and that we are put on the thorny road of this life in order to find our way, through faith and good works, back to God. That was the very fiber of which the heroic soul of Saint Birgitta was woven. And it was exactly this soul that fascinated and attracted the other saints, popes, kings, artists, explorers and men of work, who all felt like her knights in waiting. It is her spirit that permeated the centuries and, moving through history and legends, reached an almost mythological proportion — a phenomenon which can be attributed to man's need to identify himself with the most beautiful, greatest and saintliest. As Theseider states in his *History of Rome,* "Saint Birgitta . . . was certainly one of the greatest religious women who ever lived."

✧ ✧ ✧

ANIMA EROICA

The plague reared up like a fiery horse
       and galloped through country and town.
Black, virile death rode with it —
       trampling Europe down.
War, war, war —
       that first-heard cannons' roar.
Revolts, the French and English,
       the Turks. War after war.
All virtue was choked, the damned went to hell,
And the good to desolate night.
The world was a forest, a wild, dark forest,
And the candle no longer burned bright.

O what did you want from this worldly life,
Be you prince or priest or a poor peasant's wife?

To have some money; to live well, my friend;
To be honored, esteemed; a fine show at the end.

The candle burned low in the window alone,
And few people cared how dimly it shone.

Stupor et mirabilia audita sunt in terra nostra.
Strange things have been heard in our land,
But none more strange than the still small voice
From the cloud above Birgitta's shoulder
That told her:

Thou shalt be My bride. My friends resemble birds.
They fly from bush to bush, ashamed to serve Me,
Deaf to My words.
Through thee I will speak to the world.
Go to the sick, go to the poor,
Go to the king, go to the shrine.
I will guide you, My bride, My pilgrim.
Thou art Mine.

In revelations she foresaw the marriage
That would end the war.
She saw the popes return to Rome,
The straits fall to the Turks,
The Vatican become the Church's home.
She saw reforms and unity
And knew she would not fail.
She saw her spirit win;
She saw her Christ prevail.

Angel of Rome and Mystic of the North,
Call us forth
As holy knights,
And knights are dear unto His sight,
As noble knights
Who rouse to action for the right,
Who strive in the present age
To save our heritage,
Each one an anima eroica,
Like you an anima eroica,
A united heroic spirit that would
Transform the world through love and brotherhood.

MERRILL SPARKS

BIBLIOGRAPHY
The Religious and Knightly Order of St. Birgitta

Adalsten, K., Licht aus dem Norden, Fribourg, 1951

Adlerfeldt, G., De Ordinibus equestribus, Stockholm, 1696

Anrep, G., Svenska adelns ättar-taflor, Stockholm, 1864

Antoninus, St., Chronica Antonini, Lugduni, 1543

Ashmole, E., The Institution, Laws and Ceremonies, London, 1672

Auclair, M., St. Teresa of Avila, London, 1953

Ballerini, R., St. Brigida, Roma, 1895

Bång, J., Ulfspärre Ätten, Stockholm, 1741

Bar, M., Ordres Religieux et Militaires, Paris, 1756

Binet, E., La Vie de Ste. Brigitte, Lille, 1634

Birgitta zu Münster, Der Hlg. Phillip Neri, Freiburg, 1951

Bisogni, E., La sacra e nobile Milizia di S. Brigida, Roma, 1950

Brou, A., The Ignatian Way to God, Milwaukee, 1952

Buonani, F., Ordini religiosi e militari, Venezia, 1697

Burlamacchi, G., Vita di S. Brigida di Svezia, Napoli, 1692

Butkovich, A., Anima Eroica, Los Angeles, 1968

Butkovich, A., Iconography of St. Birgitta, Los Angeles, 1969

Butler, E. C., Benedictine Monasticism, London, 1919

Cahier, Ch., Caracteristiques des Saints, Paris, 1867

Cento, E., All'ombra della Croce, Roma, 1959

Chiminelli, P., La Mistica del Nord, Roma, 1948

Clark, H., A concise history of Knighthood, London, 1794

Clarus, L., Leben und Offenbarungen, Regensburg, 1856

Clerissac, H., The spirit of St. Dominic, London, 1939

Cnattingius, H., Studies in the Order of St. Bridget, Uppsala, 1963

Collijn, J., Iconographia Brigittina, Stockholm, 1918

Cornell, H., The Iconography of the Nativity, Stockholm, 1924

Coronelli, A., Ordinum Equestrum ac Militarum, Venezia, 1715

Crollalanza, Enciclopedia araldica cavallerescha, Roma, 1877

Cuomo, R., Ordini cavallereschi, Roma, 1780

Dahlberg, E., Suecia antiqua e hodierna, Stockholm, 1690

Dictionnaire des dictionnaires, Paris, 1889

Dictionnaire d'Histoire et de Géographie, Paris, 1912

Ekwall, S., Birgittavita, Stockholm, 1965

Encyclopédie Catholique, Paris, 1842

Felder, H., The Ideals of St. Francis, New York, 1925

Fenicia, G., Milizia sacra di S. Brigida, Napoli, 1862

Ferraironi, F., Il Santuario di S. Brigida, Roma, 1934

Feuerstein, H., Matthias Grünewald, Bonn, 1930

Flavigny, de C., Sainte Brigitte de Suéde, Paris, 1910

Fogelklou, E., St. Birgitta, Stockholm, 1941

Frederici, A.M.O., Diplomatarium Nobilium, Villenoy, 1913

Galante, G. A., Guida sacra della citta di Napoli, Napoli, 1883

Gardner, E. G., The story of Florence, London, 1903

Genouillac, de., Dictionnaire de Chevalerie, Paris, 1891

Gersonius, J., De Theologia mystica, Cologne, 1483

Gesta Gothorum, Gothstadt, 1940

Gill, J., Eugenius IV., London, 1961

Giustiniano, A., Annali della Republica di Genova, Genova, 1835

Giustiniano, B., Ordini militari e cavallereschi, Venezia, 1672

Graf, D., Revelations and prayers of St. Bridget, London, 1928

Grisar, H., La casa di S. Brigida, Roma, 1895

Haller, J., England and Rome unter Martin V., Rome, 1905

Hamilton, A., Angel of Syon, London, 1905

Hammerich, F., Den Helige Birgitta, Oslo, 1911

Heidenstam, V.v., Heliga Birgittas pilgrimsfärd, Stockholm, 1901

Helm, M., Birgitta von Sweden, München, 1916

Hermant, J., Histoire des Ordres de Chevalerie, Rouen, 1692

Hilton, W., The Scale of Perfection, London, 1908

Hilton, W., The Song of Angels, London, 1910

Holmgren, A. M., Heliga Birgitta, Stockholm, 1922

Hoving, J., Gothic Golden Griffin Order, Gothstadt, 1939

Horn, G., Commilitiones Christi, Stockholm, 1937

Jacob, E. F., The Fifteenth Century, Oxford, 1961

Jansen, M., Papst Bonifatius IX, Freiburg, 1904

Jean, J., Ste. Brigitte de Suéde, Paris, 1890

Johnston, F. R., The Cult of St. Bridget in XV Century, Manchester, 1947

Johnston, F. R., Blessed Richard Reynolds, London, 1961

Jørgensen, J., Saint Bridget of Sweden, New York, 1954

Kempis, Th. à., The Imitation of Christ, London, 1935

Klemming, E. E., Hlg. Birgittas Uppenbarelser, Stockholm, 1884

Knowles, D., The Religious Orders in England, Cambridge, 1859

König, E., Kardinal Giordano Orsini, Freiburg, 1906

Kranz, G., Politische Heilige, Augsburg, 1964

Lindblom, A., Life of St. Brigitta, Stockholm, 1908

Lindblom, A., Den Heliga Birgittas Bilderwerk, Stockholm, 1918

Lobkowitz, J., Theologia regularis, Lyon, 1665

Löfström, K., Sweriges Riddarordnar, Stockholm, 1948

Lunden, T., Himmleska Uppenbarelser, Malmö, 1957

Magnino, B., S. Brigida di Svezia, Roma, 1939

Magnus, O., Vita S. Catharinae, Roma, 1550

Maigne, W., Les Ordres de Chevalerie, Paris, 1891

Mancini, A., S. Brigida di Svezia, Milano, 1960

Marquez, M. J., Cavalleria antiqua e moderna, Madrid, 1642

Mendo, A., De Ordinibus militaribus, Madrid, 1671

Mollat, G., Les Papes d'Avignon, Paris, 1949

Moreau, A., Der Wanderer auf der Via Apia, Heidelberg, 1964

Moroni, G., Dizionario storico-ecclesiastico, Venezia, 1840

Nicola, G. de., Vita e Rivelazioni di S. Brigida, Napoli, 1883

Nyberg, T., Birgittinische Klöstergründungen, Leiden, 1965

On. de Santa Maria, La Cavalleria antica e moderna, Brescia, 1751

Oquendo, M., Vida di S. Brigida, San Sebastian, 1636

Panofsky, E., Early Netherlandish Painting, Cambridge, 1953

Paraiso, V., St. Bridget of Sweden, London, 1922

Passareni, L., Gli Alberti di Firenze, Firenze, 1869

Peacey, E., Saint Bridget of Sweden, London, 1933

Pedretti, C., Leonardo, London, 1973

Perrot, A., Collection historique, Paris, 1820

Pourrat, P., Spiritualité chretienne, Paris, 1924

Provvisioni, No. 128., Archivio di Stato, Firenze, 1437

Potthast, A., Biblioteca Historica Medii Aevi, Berlin, 1896

Ravaldi, N., Translation S. Catharinae Vadstensis, Uppsala, 1833

Renda, A., Il pensiero mistico, Milano, 1902

Riant, P., Scandinaves en Terre Sainte, Paris, 1851

Ribet, J., La Mystique Divine, Paris, 1879

Russo, F., Santa Brigida nella legenda, Lanciano, 1913

Sales, F. de., The Love of God, London, 1931

Schiappacasse, N., S. Brigida e Alfonso Pecha, Genova, 1904

Schiller, H., Den heliga Birgitta av Vadstena, Stockholm, 1944

Schönebeck, A., Histoire des Ordres de Chevalerie, Amsterdam, 1692

Söderblom, N., Birgitta och Reformationen, Uppsala, 1916

Stiernman, A., Svecia illustris, Uppsala, 1800

Stolpe, S., Die Offenbarungen der Hlg. Birgitta, Frankfurt, 1961

Stolpe, S., Die Frau Birgitta lächelt, Frankfurt, 1956

Stolpe, S., Das Mädchen von Orleans, Frankfurt, 1958

Stomberg, A., A History of Sweden, New York, 1931

Surius, L., Commentaries, Rome, 1535

Tenzel, W., Monatliche Unterredungen, Berlin, 1697

Theseider, D., I Papi di Avignone, Firenze, 1939